how to be a surfer

kelly Slater

Original Title: Livro 7 – Como ser surfista
© by João De Macedo & Prime Books

Dedicated to my father Jorge and my mother Luisa

British Library Cataloguing in Publication Data
A catalogue record for this book is available from the British Library

João De Macedo
how to be a surfer
Oxford: Meyer & Meyer Sport (UK) Ltd., 2007
ISBN: 978-1-84126-201-7

© 2007 by Meyer & Meyer Sport (UK) Ltd.
Aachen, Adelaide, Auckland, Budapest, Graz, Johannesburg,
New York, Olten (CH), Oxford, Singapore, Toronto
Member of the World
Sports Publishers' Association (WSPA)
www.w-s-p-a.org
Printed and bound by: B.O.S.S Druck und Medien GmbH, Germany
ISBN: 978-1-84126-201-7
E-Mail: verlag@m-m-sports.com
www.m-m-sports.com

HOW TO BE A SURFER

João De Macedo

Meyer & Meyer Sport

PREFACE

"Seldom in my years traveling the globe, have I seen a person so pure, charismatic and enthusiastic about anything he touches: Surf competitor, surf coach, president of an environmentally-orientated surf club, contributing journalist to surf magazines, and the good Soul and Inspiration to his young and aspiring Surfers – João De Macedo, a role model and friend to my son and so many others for his scholastic and athletic achievements".

Roman S. von Rupp

Yvon Chouinard, a friend and pioneer in the field of mountaineering and rock climbing, a man who over the years has excelled at almost every outdoor sport known to man, once told me, "Surfing is the purest sport on the planet."

I agree, to the extent of being bold enough to say that: "There is no greater sport in the world than that of surfing, the act of riding and performing on waves." Because when it comes to combining complex technique, strength, endurance, flexibility, courage, bravado, style and, above all in my opinion, pure enjoyment, surfing has no equal. The intensity of connection and involvement with the most powerful forces of nature are what most distinguish surfing from all other sports. As Yvon put it, the purity of the connection with each wave is unsurpassable.

how to be a surfer describes and explains a lot about modern wave performance, and the rising role of surf coaches in helping surfers perfect and refine their performance levels. But most importantly, João hasn't forgotten the golden rule that everyone involved in teaching surfing, from beginner to WQS ripper, must understand: to surf a wave is to ride the unbridled energy of a storm. So you can't just think about technique, passing heats or beating your opponent, you have to never forget that you are connecting with a superior force. When you are prepared to challenge yourself to ride bigger waves, you will feel the wholeness and communion of your being with nature in an especially intense form.

Even for a beginner, the experience of sitting on a board for the first time, among the breaking waves, is an unforgettable experience. You have suddenly become part of an environment that most people do not have the opportunity to enjoy. Out amongst the local sea creatures, viewing the shore from an oceanic viewpoint, feeling the pulse of swell under your board and the smell of salt in the air; these are of greater therapeutic value than 100 hours on the psychiatrist's couch. And when you catch your first wave? There are no words that can adequately describe the rush of that first ride; it is a memory that will last an entire lifetime.

To me, a surfer for almost thirty years, surfing is a necessary component to a happy life. Life's problems seem to roll off my back like water off a duck. And why? In our modern world, ruled by automobiles, email, cell phones, and cubicles, we are increasingly disconnected with the elemental forces that rule the planet.

Surfing in some strange way rekindles the primordial fire and reminds us of the beauty of life on Earth.

The sport of surfing has come a long way since its beginnings in ancient Hawaii. Once the sport of Hawaiian kings, it was later frowned upon by the right-minded Christian missionaries who helped to colonize the islands, viewed as a frivolous (and naked) pastime that stood in the way of the strict teachings of their religion. Later on, during its rebirth in the 1950s and '60s in America, society still viewed it generally as a waste of time. Seen as a selfish and hedonistic activity enjoyed mostly by deadbeats and bums, most people viewed it as a way to cop out on a responsible, productive life, firmly contrary to the morals of mainstream society.

How things change. The simple act of riding waves brings smiles, health, and happiness to millions of people across the globe. Many longtime and experienced surfers will tell you that, to them, surfing is more than a sport; it is a lifestyle with religious qualities.

My passion for surfing has led me across the globe in pursuit of fresh places to surf. All surf spots, all continents, all oceans and storms produce different conditions for surfing. Much like sampling a new cuisine, surf travel offers the opportunity to experience new flavors of wave, while at the same time the chance to learn more about the world's cultures. Every wave is different, and a surfer's thirst is unquenchable.

On one of my voyages, I met a surfer who I feel is truly one of our sport's greatest ambassadors. A surfer with great strength of character and a generous heart, he has a remarkable ability to teach our beloved sport to both experts and beginners alike. João De Macedo has been a coach to some of Europe's best surfing talent and has managed to boil down the essence of surfing into a format that we all can understand. *how to be a surfer* is a remarkable accomplishment and asset to surfing. Novices, professional surfers, and surf coaches will all find it an essential tool to improving their performance and enjoyment of the sport.

Through all my travels and years spent in the water, I have learned that surfers have a unique perspective in regard to nature and the preservation of our world's most vast and powerful resource: the ocean. *how to be a surfer* teaches us how to enjoy and respect the sea: how to read its many moods, enhance our enjoyment in it, and how to give something back to ensure the ocean's future health. Whatever kind of surfer you may be, no matter what tool you use to ride waves, you will find that this book will improve your surfing and might even alter your perspective on the world around you.

William Henry

William Henry is the Executive Director of the Save the Waves Coalition, a successful freelance photographer, an avid surfer and explorer, married and is the father of three children. His favorite move is pushing his quad-fin surfboards to ride round, hollow barrels.

Thank you:

I'd like to start by thanking my wife Joana and my sister Aninhas for their creative energy, enduring love and continuous search for truth and meaning. Crucial "I Ching" sessions I believe helped us all connect to our superior being and keep pushing for self-improvement.

Daniel "Rosy" Rosario, my long time friend, hard-core worker and dedicated surfer… "O Glossario do Rosario" marks but a small portion of what Daniel has contributed to this project. Obrigadao meu!!

how to be a surfer team: Mario, Will, Devon, Patrick, Carlos, and Ricardo for believing and investing energy in the project.

The San Francisco – Santa Cruz nucleus of friends: Stephan, Alex and Kai; Will and Jane; Crazy Fininho and Capoeira Megan; Andy; Gonzo Emile, Sky, Rosy, Steve…

The Aachen team: Mr. and Mrs. Meyer for their support and hospitality, Thomas, Andrea and the Meyer & Meyer Sport staff for their patience and commitment to high standards.

My friend Pedro "Noralz" Noronha and the friends of the forum: Joao "Xon Lee" Lima; Vasco "Bohemian Executive" de Castro; Dany "Fruity Style" Ernst; Joe "Cool" Ernst; Afonso "Fonsi" O'Neill; Luis "Jungle-Boy" Costa; Fred "the Fin" Vitzthum; Carl "del Rum" Edlund; Miguel "Big" Costa; Andre "Neighbour" Barroso for their support.

Barry Eichengreen, Heather Hitchner and Sarah Malarkey for their publishing insights.

Ben Marcus, Matt Warshaw and John Bain for surf literary inspiration.

Tiago, Rob, Reuben, Joao, Dave, Tomas, Nicolau, Francisco, Justin, Marlon, Tinga, Ryan, Alex, Ze, Stefan and Pecas inspirational surfers and friends.

My friend and agent Roman S. von Rupp and family: Isabel, Raphael and Nicolau.

Alfredo, Pipa, Manel e Andre Laranjinha for the support, artistic and sport know-how.

Jim and Carol DeNardo for making Joana and me feel so at home by remembering and sharing my U.S. roots.

The Portuguese San Diego crew: Xico and Manu, Ze Maria and Ana, Ze Valagao for the good times and feeling at home in SoCal.

ISA President, Board, collaborators and members: Fernando Aguerre, Maile Aguerre, Alan Atkins, Layla Marcille and Mike Gerard, Juca de Barros, Robin de Kock.

At Quiksilver: Jeff Booth and Tim Richardson for making it happen…at Channel Islands: Travis and Rick for pulling it off; at Volcom: Troy Eckert and Tom Carey for the sick photos…thanks also to Scott Daley at BodyGlove for giving it a shot!

João De Macedo

Contents

Introduction

Photo: AJ Neste / Surfing America

USA Surf Team member Karina Petroni showing power and style during the Quiksilver/ISA World Junior Surfing Championships in Tahiti.

What does being a surfer mean? How do you train to be a pro-surfer? What is the role of the surf coach in the growth and depth of surfing?

how to be a surfer poses these questions not to attempt to arrive at final or dogmatic answers, but to shed light on how America's surfing and surfers can react to the sport's needs concerning its future growth.

Coaches, judges, event organizers, business people, surf school managers and basically *all* experienced "wave sliders"and ocean dwellers have a major role and responsibility when developing the sport to also create awareness towards surfing's lifecycle commitments to the waves and the sea.

Based on the will to work towards the sustainable development of surfing, it is useful to comprehend how other sports function. Focusing on the potential depth of surfing as a sport, **how to be a surfer** has followed the concept of the sport "performance pyramid." The pyramid has various levels and, for a team or an individual to consistently reach its apex, all levels must be solidly connected.

Photo: Quicksilver

One of America's hottest up-and-coming surfers, Dane Reynolds, flies over a wave.

America already has hundreds – probably thousands – of grass-roots surfing institutions and organizations, such as the Ocean City New Jersey High School Surf Team or the Windandsea Surf Club, at the bottom of the pyramid. Their goals are diverse and vary from school to school and club to club, but they are certainly geared to some extent to scout for local talents through inter-scholastic contests and local club contests, as well as to teach basic environmental education, ocean awareness, organize beach clean-ups, etc.

These nuclear organizations must be widespread, well organized, well run and with a local focus – they are led by generally unsung heroes and make up a critical component of the pyramid: its foundations. These local organizations depend on competent judges, as well as experienced surf coaches and business people, to organize and nurture various amateur competitions – the NSSA local conference contests are a level slightly above local beach surf club's contests but are an excellent example of the level that approaches the top-end of this section of the pyramid.

Being a member of the USA Surf Team and being part of the annual National Scholastic Surfing Association (NSSA) finals at Lower Trestles is a good example of preparing the transition to a higher section of the pyramid where athletes meet and surf professionally with the best of their *country*. At this level – NSSA finals and USA Surf Team honors – the only major distinction between the National Professional level is the prize money at the contests because the level of surfing and many of the company endorsements for the best competing athletes are the same in a top Regional (e.g.: NSSA finals) and a National Professional level contest. This overlapping characteristic is important to help smoothen the always rough transition from one level to the next.

So only a small separation exists between contests that offer prize money at the Regional and National Professional level, and the NSSA and Surfing America USA Championships contests that don't offer prize money. Besides a basically equivalent level of surfing, these levels have another common trait, which is all contests are held on home soil. So the Regional WQSs (1 to 3 Star) and the "big" WQSs (4 to 6 star) hosted on home soil are also considered to be at the National Professional level. Although these "big" WQS contests attract international talent and are extremely competitive, they are hosted in the U.S. and serve as a stepping stone for those National Professional athletes who aim to reach the highest level – the pyramide's apex – the WCT and ISA's annual international contests. The pyramid's apex defines the elite of international surfing competition.

It may not be apparent, but to reach the highest level of competitive surfing many other players have important roles in helping athletes reach their potential. From the grass-roots local level to the top international level, these players include surf coaches/mentors, judges, business investors and event organizers; all crucial elements towards building a solid pyramid (i.e., a pyramid able to produce and nurture multiple talents that reach the apex). This means having established accreditation and education systems produces career paths that work towards a common goal: all players within the pyramid achieving the apex of their roles.

Photo: João Valente

Rob Machado performing a cutback during the mid-'90s famously televised National Bud Tour. Machado was a Bud Tour Champion before going on to place second in the world in 1995 and being a regular top-seed surfer on the ASP's World Championship Tour (WCT). He is the ultimate ambassador of California cool and style: an amazingly skilled performer – master of flow.

The surf coach is the one positioned closest to the athlete. The coach's focus is to help learn and refine advanced surfing technique, lead the athlete through a maze of amateur, projunior and pro contests, counsel and motivate athletes through teenage and adult challenges, and simply live by the values of being a surfer.

Connecting the level of a very sophisticated individual national amateur system to a competitive USA Surf Team and an international professional system has afflicted U.S. surfing for some time. The connection between the talent scouting of organized surf clubs and the NSSA Regionals, as well as Nationals and a strong USA Surf Team and to a professional system that produces multiple athletes for the top international level has only now begun to regain some momentum due to the persistent and serious work of Surfing America.

In the 18th century, sailors and western adventurers described the Hawaiian indigenous act of surfing.

The continuity of this important work increasingly depends on Surfing America's competence and ability to provide education and careers for judges and coaches. Just as important is the ability of the business community to support the USA Surf Team and the organization of more 4, 5 and 6 Star International WQSs on home soil.

The U.S. has the greatest champions of all-time and one of the strongest professional records of any nation, so understanding the weak spots within the pyramid has not been a major revolution in the American surfing world; it has been about refining the existing structure and the connections between the various levels of the pyramid.

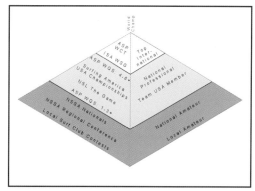

A well-functioning sport pyramid is an ideal structure for helping aspiring pro surfers learn the ropes of handling competitive pressure and performing in competition.

Surfing America and the National Surfing League (NSL) are at the forefront of these changes, contributing to more national awareness and media attention towards professional and high-performance surfing. New surfers, new competition and an invigorated responsibility for surf coaches will greatly contribute to the refinement of the sport's performance pyramid, internal organization and depth.

Clay Marzo from Hawaii deep inside a wave. The barrel – riding inside the wave – is considered surfing's ultimate move. It celebrates the surfer's intimate connection with nature.

how to be a surfer came into being by studying how surfers' most simple act of riding waves is also a complex art form. *The 7,* which refers to learning advanced surfing by perfecting 7 fundamental surfing moves, was born from a training program developed with my Surf Academy's brightest students: Nicolau Von Rupp, Pedro Pinto, Francisco Laranjinha and Tomas Valente.

Nicolau – the strongest member of our academy's advanced surfing group – has revealed himself as the most competitive surfer of the group. He has been progressing through the junior ranks to now be considered a world-class talent. However, his interaction with his core group of friends and the speed at which this group of surfers was learning advanced surfing techniques was instrumental in our coaching sessions and the refinement of *the 7*.

By focusing on specific moves of *the 7,* advanced surfers like Nicolau, Pedro, Francisco and Tom had access to objective, individual surfing goals and a long-term structure to keep perfecting their surfing techniques.

Witnessing these up-and-coming surfers reach their surfing potential and have the tools to work towards achieving their dreams solidified my confidence in *the 7*. This coaching method would later go on to be recognized and endorsed by the International Surfing Association.

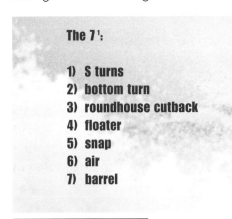

The 7 [1]:

1) **S turns**
2) **bottom turn**
3) **roundhouse cutback**
4) **floater**
5) **snap**
6) **air**
7) **barrel**

Photos: Tom Carey/ Volcom

[1] NOTE: The take-off counts as *Maneuver 0*. The *choice of wave* (after a *correct, objective assessment of the size and pulse of the surf discussed in Chapter 1*) is not counted either. Just like knowledge of *surfboards*, the *choice of wave* is part of the essential learning that accompanies surfers throughout the advanced phase of their development.

Talented 10-year-olds, like Zeze, or skilled 13-year-olds, like Coco Ho, show how advanced moves can be learned and refined at a very young age. Yet, a certain degree of maturity in and out of the water is what makes a surfer a solid professional as an adult.

Nicolau von Rupp represents the global talent that is popping everywhere:
from Europe to Mexico to Indonesia to Peru and Japan, hot young surfers are "turning heads."

Photo: Carlos Pinto

Visualizing and executing *the 7* with power, speed, risk, creativity and flow, means high-performance surfing is being learned and applied. *The 7* follows the benchmarks of performance surfing set by the ASP (Association of Surfing Professionals), and the ISA (International Surfing Association) judging criteria: "executing radical maneuvers of high difficulty and technical quality in the most critical sections of the wave with power and speed, in order to maximize the wave's potential. Innovative, progressive surfing will be taken into account when executed in a determined, controlled fashion. Surfers who abide by these criteria with the greatest degree of difficulty and control in the best waves should be awarded the highest points (on a 0 to 10 scale).[2]"

The purity and antiquity of surfing's most fundamental act (i.e., catching and riding a wave) is usually concealed by the modern developments in surfers' technique, equipment, places surfed, and waves challenged. This sport has evolved from an exclusive cultural, athletic and recreational activity of the ancient Polynesian[3] aristocracy to an internationally competitive sport adopted by many of the world's countries.

---

[2] ISA Rule Book 2006

[3] Captain Cook's accounts of his exploration of the Pacific in the late 18th century are the first and most famous descriptions of this incredible feat on the waves. There are many other stories from explorers and adventurers in the Pacific in the 18th and 19th centuries, who discovered the first surfers in the islands of Polynesia. At the time, the Polynesians joyfully performed extraordinary exercises on the waves to the amazement of the explorers. They were the first to regard riding the ocean's surf as a form of leisure and a way of communing with nature and their own being. In ancient Polynesian culture, only members of the local royal families or aristocracy could be surfers. It was Hawaiian society and its elite that took surfing much further.

Photo: Devon Howard

Dan Malloy's classic bottom turn on a classic board. The bottom turn was a revolution in the way surfers turn on a wave made possible only due to the innovations in the '60s and '70s concerning board shapes and fin configurations.

Yet even today this "sport of kings" as it is fondly known, continues to have a direct connection to nature's power and flow. This connection is the essence of its unique sportive characteristics, which balance technique with physical power, patience, creativity and courage. The sport of surfing nowadays can be about simply standing up and riding a wave[4] or, as pro surfers have proven, can also be about pushing the limits and riding deep inside waves, flying over, and carving waves of all sizes everywhere, from the Pacific to Thailand to Russia!

[4] See Glossary.

DVD: Tito da Costa

The S turns-bottom turn sequence, everything starts here. Latent in this move combination is the surfers' ability to connect the 7.

Photo: Will Henry

San Francisco's Ocean Beach shows its power. When the swell increases, the surfer understands his humble existence before nature. The search for harmony (instead of domination) with the ocean, an infinitely potent entity, is the solution.

Photos: Will Henry

Troy Brooks S turning and pulling into the barrel at Sunset Beach, Hawaii. S turns are crucial for generating speed and seem like an apparently simple move. Check out the subtle inside-to-outside rail changes, the back-to-front foot-weight transitions and the crucial arm and leg movements that make the S turns a definitely complex, yet essential move. Good surfing is impossible without speed.

Photos: AJ Neste/ Surfing America

USA Surf Team member Dane Ward shows how the 7, specifically the cutback, comes in an almost infinite number of forms. The roundhouse cutback is the base for challenging the surfer to maintain speed and rail control throughout his turns.

The USA Surf Team has finally re-achieved its importance in America's surfing consciousness. Surf coaches will have a fundamental role in both the future of Surfing America's Team USA and the NSL's "The Game" competitive format.

I believe that many of the more advanced competition surfers have spontaneously adopted an ancestral ideology, which is different from the indigenous roots of surfing in the ancient cultures of the Pacific.[5]

Kai da Silva, this book's cartoon hero, will develop techniques and his self, throughout the chapters – from micro-grom to young zen master.

The Greeks founded the Olympic Games and the sporting principles – present in all globally competitive sports – of Kalos Kagathos. This age-old philosophy is based on the values of:

1) beauty and aesthetics (in the athlete's technique and movements)
2) love and respect (for the athlete's skill and talent)
3) determination (drive to win)
4) happiness (inherent in experiencing the results of physical and mental effort)

Women in the post-millenium era have truly found their own style and form of flowing with waves. Now everywhere you can see ladies surfing, competing and having fun.

---

[5] The famous speeches by Chief Papalagui recorded in the late 19th century created the basis for the interpretation of Western culture and its interaction with nature by one of the last Indians in the islands of Polynesia. Western culture has a lot to learn from this interpretation, which is very similar to the descriptions of the Indians in North America when they were invaded, conquered and persecuted by the white men, who were ignorant of harmonious interaction with nature.

Kai's reccuring dream symbolizes the necessary steps to ascend to surfing's ideal of harmony: a dragon-sized infinite rainbow barrel.

The traditional university classroom and the dynamic, primordial relationship of teacher and student. Surfing hasn't become a team sport at the college level, but it seems like a natural step to officially be part of the NCAA (National Collegiate Athletic Association).

These values underline all competitive activities. Bruce Hopping[6], President of the Kalos Kagathos Foundation[7], is one of the people who have most stressed this new spirit and philosophy in surfing. Bruce was the first to point out how the competitive ideology of Kalos Kagathos was complementary and in harmony with the ancient roots of surfing in Hawaii and Polynesia.

Surfing is an emotional and instinctive sport. This means that while teaching and training, a surf coach should *ALWAYS* avoid hindering a surfer's creativity and freedom. This free attitude should be balanced with discipline to help athletes achieve their potential and perfect higher levels of performance.

Stimulating individual effort, respect and discipline in surfers, while keeping friendships and team environments functional demands a lot from surf coaches. It reaches to such an extent that the coaches' role goes far beyond simple technical instruction. There is a responsibility towards helping athletes reach their potential and become champions but also to develop as people – to develop as surfers who respect other surfers and also help protect the ocean and its waves. *Being a surfer* is more than just being an athlete, it is constant quest to perfect an art form and a lifestyle.

Florida's Damien Hobgood charges the barrel during the Quiksilver Pro in Fiji. In the barrel – the fall is eminent, hit by the lip or pulled too deep into an aquatic spiral. Survival and success on the wave depends on balance.

---

6 Bruce is also the patron of the International Surfing Association (ISA), an organizer of international exchanges between surfers, and a philanthropist.

7 The Kalos Kagathos Foundation is based in San Diego, California. In Greek, kalos means "physical beauty" and kagathos means "man's spiritual and moral perfection."

Photo: Carlos Pinto

The modern beach classroom! Introductory surf courses help people be safer in the ocean, understand surf etiquette and learn basic surfing techniques.

Surfers can benefit tremendously from the help and support of a top-quality surf coach. Increasingly, surfers and surf teams resort to the guidance of coaches. Surf coaches themselves require special training, experience and a favorable context to work in (i.e., the functional sport pyramid). Coaching quality is primarily based on experience and on recognized coaching credentials. These two factors are essential for aspiring surf coaches and the surf schools or camps they are affiliated with.

The positive effect of quality education applies to any human activity, including surfing. I understand that the efforts and successes of surf coaches and surf schools around the world are a unique opportunity for this book to be in harmony with the need to establish standards of teaching quality and to provide credible, practical information about the essential steps in a surfer's technical, physical, competitive and mental development.

How far can surf coaches and surf schools help young athletes develop? Can they lead to the point of learning and refining radical moves like this one by Clay Marzo? The answer is YES! Alone or with your coach, you just need the will to learn and train your moves, without stifling your spontaneity or creativity.

Photo: Quiksilver

Photo: Will Henry

The simple act of surfing is the basis of all education in surf schools and camps. As such, the mystic harmony with nature is an essential message for coaches to transmit and repeat. Moments like these, of surf and aquatic illusion, nourish the mystery surrounding the act.

It is only from more educated members of a culture that we can demand more consideration and individual responsibility. Education is the key.

My hope in surfing is that the simple, humble act of catching a wave will always serve as an example of how sport in society reminds us of the need for harmony, peace, perseverance, respect and the pursuit of excellence in achieving true human progress. The need for a non-violent interaction is a fundamental objective, which all surfers must learn and pursue, if the surfing world is to truly be an example of an alternative and balanced lifestyle.

Photo: Will Henry

A North Californian beachbreak shows its magic. Moments like this help us tune into (instead of attempting to dominate) nature. The perspective and attitude of the surfer represents the search for the underlying beauty in harmony.

The Stages in the Life of the Cartoon Hero "Kai da Silva"

A surfer's life, just like that of any living being, goes through several periods throughout its lifecycle. The cartoon character Kai da Silva illustrates the phases and stages in life and of being a surfer. Kai manages throughout his life to develop his technique and his way of thinking and living in society.

Achieving and maintaining *balance, fluidity* and *harmony* with nature and its waves are the most spontaneous aspects of surfing. To be or not to be fluid and balanced is the essential, permanent decision in Kai's life.

During his life-long search *to be a surfer,* Kai will be accompanied by his family, friends and coach, as well as mystical symbols and decisions. We will follow his life from the beginning, through his teens, until his transition into a young adult.

Kai da Silva, the surfer, has to conquer his own style and attitude. He is going to learn that, with a little effort, in addition to coming closer to nature, he can extend this goal of fluidity and channel it to relations with other people.

Kai's total involvement in a constantly changing environment is a metaphor representing a lifestyle that is always changing.

Kai lives the life of *being a surfer* to the fullest, he is the hero illustrating the ideal of being.

At best, **how to be a surfer** is intended to make a real contribution to the *education* of surfers everywhere. Implementing the measures that support a strong and positive "performance pyramid" is a long-term process that has to be followed by many individuals. We have tried to establish a sincere, practical link between our readers and the roots of surfing and sports as the way of understanding and stimulating surfing's unique contribution to the world.

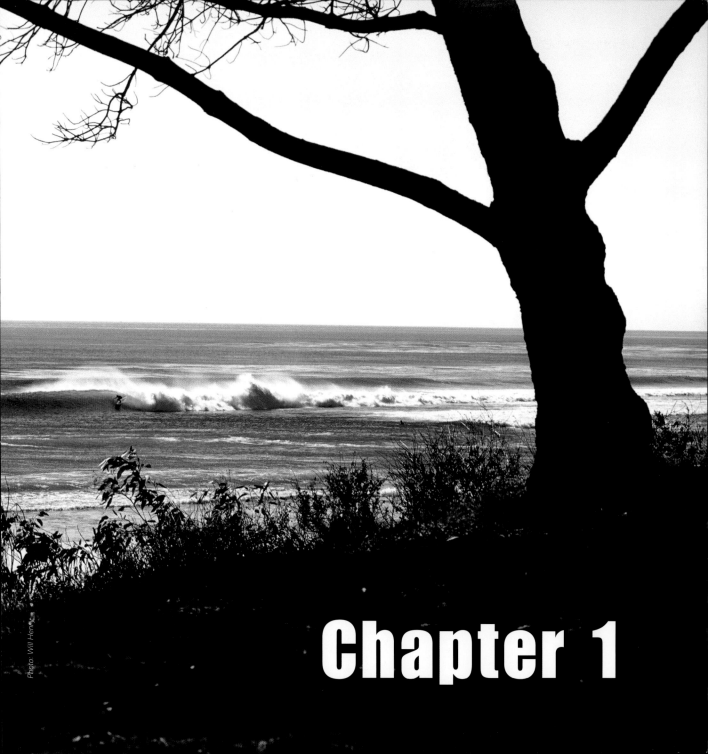

Photo: Will Henry

Chapter 1

Maverick's, California: The power of the ocean is immeasurable. Respect (never fear) is a primordial requisite for anyone who wants to be a surfer.

I've Never Even Seen the Ocean, Let Alone a Surfboard!!

Everyone's first experience with a surfboard in the ocean is usually extremely frustrating and discouraging. Many people give up after their first try. You find yourself out in the ocean, nervous with a surfboard, surrounded and pounded by waves, trying desperately to stand up on water! But it looked so easy on television…

This phase in learning tests you to the point of knowing whether you can meet these initial challenges of nature, or not. Surfers can transform apparently hostile environments into sources of energy and strength that reinforce the need to persevere and fight in life. Whatever their age, size, weight, ethnic origin or personality, surfers tend to have a positive attitude towards life.

Pipeline, Hawaii – The ultimate wave makes everyone pay attention to the pulse of the sets, the tides and the wind; before each session, experienced surfers attentively observe the conditions to improve positioning once they are in the water.

Observation and Assessment of Ocean Conditions

George – a middle-age university professor from Texas – showed up at our surf school on an unusually hot August day. He wanted a private beginner's lesson surfing course for himself and his wife it was a 25th wedding anniversary present for her.

I began the course with an introduction on how to observe and assess the sea and wave conditions. Right from the second lesson, Teresa tried particularly hard to get the sea and weather conditions right, "The wind's from the northeast today, isn't it? I think low tide is at 1:47 p.m., so in two hours the waves should be about a meter high; there aren't many rips and currents, and ... Hey, how am I doing, João?" she would ask. I was impressed by Teresa's attention to the conditions, especially her accurate assessments of the wind and tides, but noticed how, like most students, she estimated wave size too quickly.

It takes at least 10 minutes to evaluate the sea conditions properly. It is this observation time that gives us a more exact idea of the size and rhythm of the waves, which is essential information especially for beginners to surf safely.

Surf Academy Tip: *Competition surfers spend 20 minutes or more getting as much information as possible about the frequency and size of the sets[8], the right position in the water to catch the best waves, the fastest way to get through the surf, etc. So whoever you are, up-and-coming young ripper or weekend beginner, never forget to patiently observe the surf conditions.*

Basic Knowledge Regarding Surfboards

Learning about the basic characteristics of surfing equipment (i.e., the surfboards) is generally the second theoretical component of a beginner's surfing course. Unlike Teresa, George paid little attention to the observation of surf conditions but was always anxious for more details about the surfboards.

After observing the conditions, it is crucial to know the equipment necessary for catching waves. Beginner's boards are long, wide and thick: they range from 7" feet to more or less 9" in length; 19' to 20' inches wide and 2 to 3 inches thick. These board dimensions all contribute to maximizing stability in the water.

Kelly Slater's secret weapons. Knowing about equipment is essential to keep improving one's surfing technique and performance, especially once the surfer has a quiver[9] of surfboards to change and adapt to different waves and conditions.

[8] See Glossary.
[9] See Glossary.

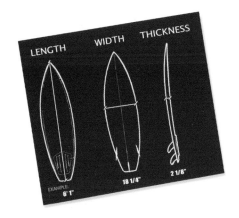

Santa Cruz legendary artist and surfer Jim Phillips subtly demonstrates that dedicated surfers have lots of surfboards!

I remember one day, George asked me, "I use a 9-ft. surfboard[10], a long board, right? But that kid's surfboard, the one who's here every day, I think he belongs to your surf club's team, must be about 5'2" or 5'4"; it's tiny! And I've seen him doing some really quick, sharp maneuvers. It must be very difficult to keep your balance on a board like that if I already have trouble on this "boat!"

Florida's Jeff Crawford at the moment living in Rocky Point, Hawaii exemplifies how a surfer's consistent connection to nature is the origin of surfing happiness. Stoke can be felt throughout the whole human lifecycle by surfers who commit themselves to be in direct contact with the infinity of the ocean and waves.

I comforted him saying that, at any level of surfing, the most important thing is to have fun and stay safe. The big, soft boards he was using served this purpose, "As you develop and refine your basic technique, you are able to surf on smaller,

---

[10] Surfboards are measured in feet and inches. Here we are talking about length, but there are other important measurements, like width and thickness, which are also in feet and inches.

tailor-made surfboards, but until you can drop down a wave with control and ideal take-off timing the bigger boards help out a lot."

Both George and Teresa were having lots of fun, so they said they wanted to carry on the following week. In fact, even after having a bit of a bad experience on one of the smaller surfboards, George still said he was going to learn to surf on them and catch and ride some real waves! Both had a great spirit!

I once had a group of teenage boys and girls from a local high school, enroll in a surfing beginner's course through their school. They were at an age where they just oozed energy.

It was interesting to notice how the details about surfboards that George (older and more mature) had found so fascinating only attracted a couple of the boys. It was also curious to understand that when it came to assessing ocean conditions, I had again to constantly stress the need to take a little more time to observe and assess the size and rhythm of the waves. The teenagers, especially the girls, were better than the boys at learning the basic details of surf observation. They, at least, invested the time to gauge the wind and tides.

Observing the conditions while getting ready to surf is a natural way of doing the right thing, which even the best follow. It is important to properly check out the conditions and verify if anyone is in the water – especially if you are on a surf trip at a remote location.

Once in the water, this group proved to be quite gutsy (or foolhardy!). Emma, one the best students of the group, knew "everything" about ocean conditions, how to assess the size of waves and understand the details about surfboards' measurements. Right from the first lesson, she wanted to get out in the water and catch unbroken waves.

YOU SHOULD'VE SEEN HIM!!

YOUR DAD RODE BARRELS WITH HIS ARMS STRETCHED OVER HIS HEAD AND THERE WAS STILL 8 FEET ABOVE HIM

YOU'RE VERY YOUNG KID; YOU SHOULD HAVE FUN, BUT GO TO SCHOOL

I WAS A GREAT FRIEND OF YOUR DAD WHEN HE WAS AROUND

EVERY NIGHT BEFORE FALLING ASLEEP KAI WOULD LOOK AT HIS BOARD AND THINK OF HIS FATHER

I NEVER SAW ANYONE WITH SUCH ATTITUDE AND STYLE

MY NAME IS PAKAL VOTAN

HE DID INCREDIBLE THINGS. I ALWAYS HAD A LOT OF ADMIRATION FOR THE HUMBLE-NESS AND WILL POWER HE SHOWED IN ALL HIS ACTIONS

YOU ARE NOT ALONE. WE WILL MEET AGAIN

FROM THEN ON, KAI'S CHILDHOOD WAS TOUCHED BY THE STORIES ABOUT HIS FATHER TOLD BY ALL THE SURFERS WHO RESPECTED HIM.

ALL OF THEM HAD ADVICE TO GIVE HIM AND IN A WAY FILLED A BIT OF THE EMPTINESS.

At first, we had to keep an eye on her to make sure she didn't get too separated from the rest of the group. She later told me that her father and brother were surfers and that she had already caught some waves with them. I tried to explain to Emma and the other more adventurous boys that, although it was important to be bold and adventurous, you have to measure the size of the waves very carefully and patiently. Respect for the ocean and correctly evaluating ocean conditions can help prepare surfers to confront difficult situations.

Environmental Awareness

In a beginner's surfing course, I also like to talk about the importance of understanding how the spirit of surfing has an active responsibility to protect nature. Surfers' contribution to education and activism is fundamental. There were contrasting feelings among this class of teenagers.

Some were clearly more pro-active, while others were more complacent. What unified the class was the practical awareness of nature's superior force and power. These kids felt strongly attracted to the power of the ocean, and they came to understand that they could help this environment just by being more conscious and aware of how there is sometimes a lack of respect towards the search for harmony with this force of nature. They comprehended that saying something about it was always better than a neutral, say/do-nothing attitude.

I couldn't help feeling that it had been useful for them to experience surfing and its close contact with nature, especially because, as teenagers, these kids were going through a phase in their lives when they were being bombarded with sensations and feelings. With surfing, they were given the opportunity to indulge in a healthy yet exciting and intense activity.

Another interesting and telling case of first-hand experiences with surfing happened when a couple in their late-thirties, enrolled in another of our surf school summer beginner courses.

Right from the first lesson, David and Inez made fun of the fact that they were so overweight! They each weighed more than 190 pounds and were both more than 6 feet tall. Their 14-year-old son Carlos was also taking classes. He already weighed 165 pounds and had reached a height of nearly 5'9!

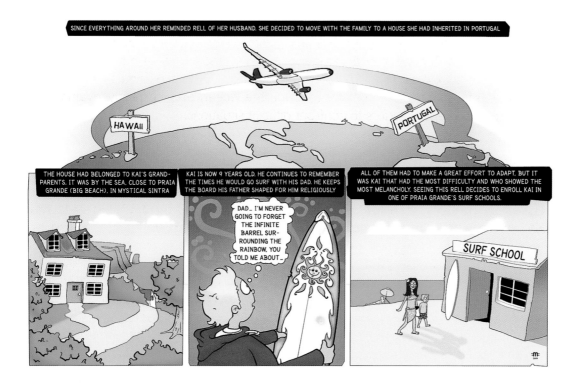

What this couple lacked in natural ability and talent, they made up for with an overwhelming joy and good attitude. Carlos was the one who paid most attention to the theoretical part of the course. On the other hand, what David and Inez wanted was to get to the practical part, out in the water. Carlos tried to teach his parents what he had learned, but they just wanted to be out in the waves!

By the end of their course, they had successfully learned to stand up and surf waves. But even after they finished taking classes, they continued to regularly show up at the beach and stimulate us to keep fostering and educating awareness towards environmental issues. It is inspiring to see how passing on the message of being more aware of forms to protect and interact with nature is a small but consistent step to being part of the solution and not the problem.

Surf Academy Tip: *So you enjoyed surfing and being in the ocean, but are you willing to help and give back? You don't need to do much to answer and act affirmatively: participate in your local beach clean-ups, help organize clean-ups, plant a tree, become a member of the Surfrider Foundation or the Save the Waves Coalition or another environmental organization that works in your local area. Be active and participate!*

The basic joy and respect of surfing has nothing to do with personal size or weight. It is all about a positive feeling towards nature. Surfing has the power to make anyone have fun and be appreciative of the ocean's power and beauty. But having a proactive attitude towards the environment is, in reality, a pretty big step taken only by some surfers. This step should be continuously emphasized by surf instructors, coaches, surf schools and camps, as well as by all experienced surfers so a difference is made and followed through.

Wave Etiquette

Regarding the importance of wave etiquette and respecting other surfers, I once witnessed a very telling case. I was surfing with Tom one of our academy's most advanced surfers. I watched him catch a perfect set wave: he pulled into the barrel right off the take off and accelerated to pass the first section and then a second one. He was going super fast in the barrel.

Just when he was coming out of the barrel, a beginner surfer from one of our afternoon classes stubbornly paddled towards the face of the wave. All experienced surfers know that doing this is dangerous and an act of disrespect for whomever is already surfing the wave.

The beginner forced Tom to jump off his board, at full speed, nearly breaking his neck. But what happened next was surprising and really positive. Tom was obviously extremely irritated but hearing the beginner repeatedly apologize, he understood how this beginner was aware he had done something stupid and regretted it. Instead of blowing up, Tom maintained his composure and explained, "Now you know why your instructors tell you to never paddle towards the open face of a wave. Always paddle towards the whitewater in case a surfer is riding the wave in front of you. You gotta be careful, you can hurt yourself and others, too. Don't be a kook."

Santa Cruz legend Peter Mel was "towed-in" by a jet ski into this giant Northern California wave. Acquiring the skills to ride big waves starts right here in this chapter! Although it takes years of experience and personal will to achieve these moments, the joy and beauty of the act is unmistakable, regardless of the size of the wave!

Photo: Patrick Tretz

This is a great example of learning wave etiquette, because experienced surfers often lose the chance to help educate people about good and safe manners in the water by sometimes getting violent and many times too quickly yelling and criticizing the shortcomings of beginners.

> **Surf Academy Tip:** *If you feel something went wrong in the water with another surfer, don't hesitate in apologizing. Even if you think you are right, communicate your concern with other surfers. Being sensitive to others and recognizing you might have messed up goes a long way in avoiding conflict. Just say (and mean it), "I am sorry." Be humble and learn something more about ocean etiquette.*

Photo: Will Henry

The waves may be perfect, but the size and the currents are less obvious. One of this chapter's main lessons is stimulating all surfers to be safe by observing and evaluating the ocean and crowd conditions before jumping in. Especially if the waves are perfect like this!

CONCLUSION

To survive (yes, to survive!), beginners have to start by learning a number of theoretical lessons that range from how to assess ocean conditions to how to recognize surfing equipment and understanding basic surfboard measurements. Learning about the correct way to paddle, "take-off" in the whitewater and manage a board in the surf are all in the second more practical part of beginner's surfing course. Chapter 2 will focus on these topics.

This chapter marks the starting point on the way to experiencing why "only a surfer knows the feeling." Reaching this feeling is the final objective of any introductory surfing course and the prize of passing the initiation that true surfing demands.

Introductory surfing courses bear the great responsibility of creating the foundations of knowledge and good attitude. These foundations should be accurate and useful and enable any beginner to learn and respect the principles of what it is *to be a surfer*. Above all, introductory surfing courses should teach beginners to feel what only a surfer feels, to respect the ocean and other surfers, and to be motivated to develop these feelings, principles and techniques as much as possible.

Every surfer I have met over the years and each student I have taught has a story to tell about this demanding initiation we covered in Chapter 1! Everyone, whether young or old, Hawaiian or Australian, big or small, goes through this phase of total ignorance of how to surf and how to act towards other surfers in the water. Learning is demanding and difficult in the ocean. So, if something goes wrong in the line-up, beginners must always apologize and more experienced surfers should try their hardest to forgive unintentional mistakes and be helpful.

All surfers tend to progressively learn how to become aware and respectful of nature's power and also of other surfers. This attitude goes a long way in making a difference in a crowded line-up. Plus, all surfers' safety and fun really depends on it!

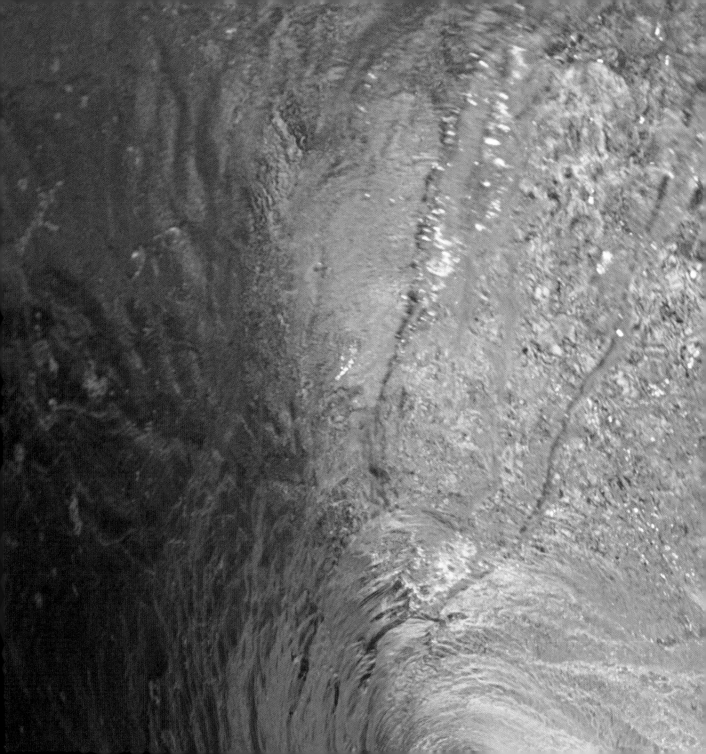

Chapter 2

The "take-off" represents move 0 in surfing. Dave Rastovich demonstrates.

I Don't Know Anything About Surfing, How am I Going to Manage?

C hapter 2 covers the practical principles of using and handling a surfboard in the waves and the most elementary technique (or move) of surfing: the "take-off," or the act of standing up on a wave.

George and Teresa showed up as arranged for another week of lessons. After their first beginner's course, they were keen to keep training and learning about surfing and the ocean.

They naturally found it difficult to use and handle their boards in the ocean while:

1) keeping their balance when paddling on the board
2) turning the board to catch waves
3) correctly executing the take-off

Sometimes they just wanted to get into the water to paddle and get a little exercise. Other times, George, more than Teresa, practiced his take-off, which was improving progressively from one session to the next. But more than anything, they both seemed pleased and at ease in an environment so immersed in nature.

Surf Academy Tip: *Once you learn how to execute a take-off, you must continue to be aware of your surfing ability and avoid going to very crowded areas in the surf. Catching many waves in a crowded situation is considered "greedy," so be patient and you'll catch your waves!*

It's very important to simulate paddling and taking-off, on the sand before attacking the waves. All surfers should have solid notions of surf etiquette and basic surfing techniques to assure safety and fun in the water.

Photo: Carlos Pinto

After training on the sand comes the actual practice in the ocean. The beginner must learn how to paddle and manage a surfboard in the water before he/she can catch waves.

Photo: Carlos Pinto

Nowadays with help from instructors and coaches, it is possible to catch a wave, stand up, and ride to shore during your first surf session. It is up to surf coaches and instructors to teach respect for the ocean.

Photo: Carlos Pinto

After riding several waves especially towards the end of the second week of classes, George continued to say only half jokingly, that he wanted to ride a small board again! So I gave in to his eagerness and let him try to ride my board. Not a good idea!

We had repeatedly gone over two basic principles of surf etiquette: showing respect and awareness towards all other people who are in the water and staying out of the way of oncoming surfers by always paddling towards the white-water of a breaking wave (never towards the "green" or open-face).

Still, accidents happen. George, by mistake, destroyed my board, scratched his arms and legs on the broken board and nearly missed an innocent swimmer! He was the first to remark that keenness doesn't substitute ability. He understood this final lesson of humbleness very well, "Will and motivation take you almost all the way, but you need respect and modesty to keep you there."

Just like David's and Inez's natural satisfaction with surfing, George's and Teresa's genuine joy emphasized what all dedicated surfers already know: you don't have to be a world champion or an extremely talented surfer to have fun in the water. Just feeling the privilege of being in close contact with the ocean is enough to be happy and aware of the essential values of *being a surfer.*

Surf Academy Tip: *It is very important for learners to catch lots of whitewater waves so that they can improve their balance and perfect their take-off. The number of waves you catch increases the speed at which you learn the one-move take-off. At this stage, quantity counts more than quality!*

When two swimming instructors from Washington, D.C., showed up at the beach, I knew that we were in for something different! Sean was 27 and Belinda was a year younger. They were tall and strong; obviously regular athletes. They were on vacation and had one more week in Portugal. They approached me and asked if they could join a beginner's surfing course. They wanted to use their remaining holiday time to learn a new sport.

Photo: Sintra Surf Association Arquives

An introduction to the basic information about surfboards and how to observe ocean conditions should be part of all introductory surf courses, like this one given by our Surf Academy to kids from an under-priviledged urban neighborhood.

In the first lesson, I dealt with the topics mentioned in Chapter 1:
1) how to gauge sea conditions and wave size
2) surfboard equipment basics
3) basic rules of wave etiquette and respect for other surfers in the water

They were interested students and did their best to learn these theoretical principles as fast as possible so that they could go out into the ocean.

The fact that they were athletes was obvious in the more physical and practical aspects of the classes. They loved paddling on their soft longboards and their experience as swimmers helped them to paddle efficiently (one arm at a time). Given these guys' paddling ability and strength, they had very little trouble getting into the right position to catch waves. They were able to control the bigger boards easily (180° turns) and could paddle for ages. They were also able to catch lots of whitewater waves and even attempt some unbroken waves.

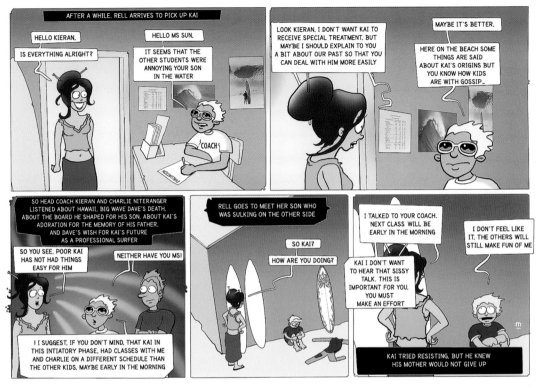

They were also very quick in learning how to duck dive[11], which is essential to pass under an oncoming wave when paddling out (see drawings and photos of the three main techniques):

1) foam ball (small) water passes between body and board

2) foam ball (big) water passes over surfer (the rollo technique)

3) traditional duck dive

DUCK-DIVING TECHNIQUES

(I.) DUCK-DIVE FOR SMALL WHITEWATER WAVE

(II.) DUCK-DIVE FOR POWERFUL WHITEWATER WAVE

(III.) TRADITIONAL DUCK-DIVE FOR WHITEWATER AND UNBROKEN WAVES

[11] see Glossary

Be it boys or girls, young or elderly, the ocean tends to transmit natural and healthy tranquility and happiness. Learning the benefits of being connected to the ocean can start very early as proven by Tom Wegener and his son Finley.

Finally, in the most important move of the course, the take-off, their agility and strength helped them to learn quicker than normal because of the number of waves they were catching per class.

Belinda managed to stand up and hold on for a few seconds in her second lesson. Although Sean found his balance during his third class, he went right ahead and dropped down an unbroken wave, riding it to the end. He was absolutely thrilled! I had to dampen his enthusiasm a little by pointing out that diving head first off the board is not a good idea!

Surf spots with sand offer the ideal conditions for a gradual and more controlled learning experience. The "outside" waves are available for the more advanced surfers and the "inside" whitewater waves are available for beginners.

It was a great experience working with these two swimming instructors. It reminded me of something that applies to all courses and classes: when it comes to picking up the basic board handling techniques and take-off technique, people in better physical condition have a tendency to learn faster (though not necessarily better).

On the day that Belinda and Sean finished their beginner's course, a group of very special novices, quite different from them, showed up. The group consisted of five children aged between 5 and 10, all very excited and ready to go surf. Their parents had important questions on the coach-student ratio, on the school's safety procedures and other issues regarding the school's normal functioning. They noticed how it is very positive for the kids to have their parents' attention. I told them how having the parents watch the first lessons of their kids in the surf gives them extra confidence.

Observation of the size and pulsation of waves at surf spots with rocks is very important to avoid accidents. Without sand or a beach, surfers must be patient and experienced to time their entry and exit in the water.

Watching the surf, timing the waves and the sets, checking the wind comes naturally to surfers when they observe the conditions.

Surf Academy Tip: *For the parents: especially with young kids, 4- to 10-year-olds, always try to take the time to watch your child's first surf class. Ask the surf school manager or instructor how many kids per coach will be in the water? What kind of experience do the surf coaches have? Can the kids be insured? These questions and your presence gives you a better idea of what and how the child is learning and, above all, it really gets the younger ones amped to perform!*

Kids can under-perform, accidents, although very rare, can happen and surfing is a tough sport that requires persistence to really learn the fundamental techniques. Therefore, you must trust and feel comfortable with the spirit and dedication of your child's school, team of instructors and surf coaches.

Belinda and Sean were impressed by the fact that it was possible to teach what they had learned to such young kids! "The more time you have to learn the basic principles, the stronger your foundations to keep developing and refining your surfing skills."

They realized that speed must also be associated with depth of learning. They were sad to be going back home. Belinda was sad because she had to go straight back to work at the swimming pools in D.C., while Sean still had some time and he was hooked: all he wanted to do now was surf!

He was going to use up his last days and savings to go to San Diego where he could carry on surfing! They said their goodbyes and set off to the airport, assuring me that from now on, wherever they went, they would always try to find some waves and a surfboard.
They were stoked!

This surfer shows all his experience in an "off the rocks" access jump. This jump gives him access to the breaking waves "outside." But after surfing the waves "outside," he is going to have to deal with the exit!

Photo: João Valente

I met another athlete shortly after the swimmers went home, a Norwegian snowboarder.

Ato is one of those individuals who has a natural gift for sports. His spontaneous demonstrations of balance were incredible, "Not even with a baseball bat could I hit him off his board!" Given his gift for sports and experience as a snowboarder, Ato's progress was fast, and he soon overcame the beginner stage. He had no trouble in paddling and mastering the agility of quick take-offs. He was starting to manage turns on the wave, but he tended to forget to keep his cool when assessing wave size, currents, wind and tide. He had the habit of never making a patient and objective evaluation of ocean conditions.

This wave looks appealing, but a closer look shows that it is big. Big waves can be perfect but their raw power is uncontrolled and merciless. The correct and pondered observation of the ocean is a necessity for surfers and the only way to evaluate the risk and prevent the dream from becoming a nightmare!

Photo: Will Henry

This lesson, focused on in Chapter 1, is very important to assure the surfer's safety in the ocean. Ato was about to learn the hard way that humility and patience define the best and most useful attitude to use when flowing with the brutal force of the ocean and its waves.

During a big, clean, summer swell, Ato didn't stop to notice the rhythm of the ocean, and he went out to show off to a group of friends who had come to visit him. He paddled out through the breaking waves easily, without realizing how big they actually were. Poor Ato didn't realize what he had gotten himself into! When the first set came, he got beaten up so badly that the lifeguards had to go out and bring him back to shore.

Ato's humbling case is a perfect illustration of the dangers even for talented surfers, of overconfidence and an impatient assessment of the waves.

Photo: Quiksilver

Brazilian surfer Peterson Rosa goes for a radical backside take-off; by paddling hard to get into the wave and then staying focused and calm all the way down it, he has a better chance of "making it."

CONCLUSION

This chapter covered the more practical techniques of learning how to surf, namely knowing how to:

1) paddle, swiftly with one arm at a time, so as to catch waves and move in the ocean

2) turn the surfboard 180 degrees, so as to position oneself to catch waves

3) duck dive waves, so as to catch bigger waves – farther away from the beach

4) take-off so as to stand up on the surfboard in one swift movement

Before beginners achieve "the feeling," nature has lessons to teach surfers to be aware of their modest existence. Overconfidence (as we saw with Ato) on the part of a talented beginner is usually instantly punished if he/she does not gauge the size of the waves, the rips and the ocean conditions, in general.

Beginners' and experienced surfers' confidence in their technique and in their strength in catching waves must not stand in the way of their judgment and respect for the ocean and other surfers. Instilling this respect, without causing fear, is one of the surf coach's main obligations. The biggest obstacle lies in the fact that these lessons of respect are learned sometimes in a fun way, other times under the pressure of an extremely unpredictable and intolerant environment, of incalculable energy. We can't forget that while the ocean demands respect, it is still the ultimate playground!

Chapter 3

Devon Howard cruisin' on his longboard: pure feeling!

"Only a Surfer Knows the Feeling"

The title of this chapter is an age-old slogan used by one of surfing's major surf companies: Billabong, Inc. Although it is used as a commercial and advertising slogan, it draws attention to a special feeling of contact and harmony with nature that surfers experience when riding waves.

Surfers know that it takes time to flow with this greater energy force and time to achieve the knowledge and practice that gives you access to this feeling. That is part of the reason surfing is such a unique sport.

Wave about to break – Learning the timing and the feel of the "sliding" motion necessary to catch and ride a wave is the secret behind achieving the "feeling."

Photo: Carlos Pinto

For those who imagine surfing as an activity linked solely to the beach, the sun, summer, and the Beach Boys, think again because you are going to have to face a lot of difficulties, obstacles and make some serious effort before you can actually surf. And for others who think surfing is a new extreme sport, nothing could be further from the truth.

Surfing has an ancient relationship with indigenous Polynesia; born hundreds or thousands of years ago as a cultural, competitive and leisure activity of the ocean-dependent tribes of the Pacific. This historic connection distinguishes surfing from all other "extreme," "outdoor," "action" or other categorizations for youth-orientated sports.

Photo: Will Henry

In such a crowded surf spot is it still possible to feel the "feeling?" The patient, devoted and perseverant surfer can only answer positively: "the feeling is with me whenever I surf. Sometimes I must stay calm and wait longer, other times I am more alone and I can indulge in catching more waves. But the bottom line is, I only need to catch one or two good waves to have a good surf."

Photos: João Valente & Will Henry

"The feeling" is normally achieved on a 1 surfer: 1 wave ratio. Dropping in on another surfer – observe photo of "dude" dropping in on the lady – is in general a rude and disrespectful act. Sometimes friends drop in on each other – see these two guys having fun on the same wave – that means sharing waves is possible but only if there is consent and a lot of skill!

Anyone who has devoted more than just a summer to surfing and has read about its history will understand what I mean. Surfing not only has history, it has a unique path to follow into the future.

Nevertheless, surfing for most people starts as a source of amusement during summer vacations. That is not a problem!

Nicolau – nowadays top member of our Surf Academy's advanced training group – was 9 years old when he decided to try surfing for the first time. He had bodyboarded but when he saw surfers performing some spectacular moves on TV he wanted to do the same. Nicolau was placed in a beginner's class, yet he ended up being part of a pioneer group of kids who like him joined the surf school during the summer. In fact, during the summer, kids all around the world enroll in surf schools. It definitely represents the best season to give surfing a try!

Nicolau's defining moment, as a surfer, occurred when he asked to use one of the school's smaller surfboards to go surf with two of our instructors. He managed to get out in the surf and catch a wave, a very important wave. He was able to take-off at just the right time, throw himself down the wave face, position himself and his board so that he was parallel to the beach and then he simply gained more speed and rode the wave's open face all the way to shore!

Surf Academy Tip: *Never give up because reaching the surfer's feeling is a challenge which is acessible to everyone. Being prepared to fall and wipe out is mostly about staying calm underwater – if you are caught by a wave – and not going head first in shallow water. Then having the will to come back and try it again!*

What came next says it all. "Did you see me, João, did you see? I was surfing!" he shouted. He was running up and down the beach with excitement! It was true: he had surfed. He successfully "slid" across a wave and consequently experienced "the feeling." Memorable seconds for Nicolau gave him one of the purest and most sublime moments in surfing.

It was his reward for being persistent and confident throughout the summer, enduring the first tests the ocean and its waves had put him through.

Nicolau and the rest of our beach's pioneer grommets got through the first stages of learning how to surf and managed to experience the feeling during the summer. But after that, whether as an athlete or not[12], there is no real end to the challenges a surfer can experience. It depends on his/her attitude, personality and will. Nicolau has gone on to prove that!

Experiencing the feeling marks a moment of transition. The surfer passes from being a beginner to being on a more advanced level of learning; a level when he/she begins to refine surfing technique.

---

[12] Regular surfing is not only a leisure activity but is also recognized as a spiritual activity.

Nicolau and Tom (see Introduction) were the early members of one of the hottest groups of young surfers to come out of our beach. Surfing became their sport and passion. We will see in Chapter 4 that they continued to progress and develop their techniques and skills to a very high level but like others before them, achieving "the feeling" was when everything really started – a successful take-off, a good trimline and access to knowing that "Only a surfer knows the feeling!"

Rebecca is a talented snowboard instructor who works during the winter on the slopes and started learning to surf in the summer. She liked the idea of travelling to warmer areas with nice beaches and good surf. So naturally she took up surfing as her second sport. She had had very little experience surfing but would show us an incredible attitude and strong will to learn and persist.

Photo: Carlos Pinto

The role of the instructor is very important to help the student learn the exact timing of the take-off.

◢◢ how to be a surfer

When she arrived at our school, Rebecca had just come from France where she had taken a pre-beginners surfing course in Biarritz. She knew how to paddle and handle the board, but was having a lot of trouble dropping down our beach's steeper waves.

Nicolau demonstrates the result of an early take-off: observe in the 3rd photo how he missed the wave.

Pedro demonstrates a slow take-off using a knee (notice the 3rd photo). The result of the take off being in two movements is the loss of precious moments at the beginning of the ride that, in more advanced stages, lead to the loss of movement potential right after the take-off. Additionally, the surfer will have serious difficulties in descending tubular or vertical waves.

Joana demonstrates a late take off, descending the wave lying down and standing up only at the base of the wave. This makes it very difficult for her to catch the open face of the wave and "slide across" it.

Jake Patterson demonstrates a textbook take-off under extreme conditions.

Taking off at the right time is what enables a surfer to drop-in and surf unbroken waves. That is the essence of the surfer's "feeling" and Rebecca was close to experiencing it.

What was holding her back was the fact that she was taking off too early and ending up behind the wave instead of catching it. It was frustrating and it was testing her determination to the fullest.

Surf Academy Tip: *To drop down into steeper waves, your take-off has to be fast and executed ideally in one swift movement/jump (no knees, no hesitation). If in doubt about the efficiency of your take-off, ask someone to film you surfing or ask your surf coach to comment on your take-off. Don't postpone correcting it because once you get bad take-off habits, it is very difficult to eliminate them. Practice at home: on the floor – one swift move; at the beach: on the sand before getting in the water – one swift move; and in the water before catching a wave – one swift move: practice makes perfect!*

Pedro also demonstrates a perfect one-movement take-off, keeping his center of gravity low, learning that in order to make the most vertical drops, you must be fast and keep your knees and legs bent throughout the descent.

Photos: Carlos Pinto

In this sequence of a wave breaking, we can witness the magic of being in tune with the end of the wave's life: a truly unique moment. To capture and intimately flow with the energy of a wave is the most holy and intense moment in surfing.

To get Rebecca through this phase, we had to help her jump onto the board at the exact moment the wave broke. So I positioned myself in the water to help her find her timing. After taking off too early, she went through a stage of taking off too late. This meant she was dropping-in on the wave lying down and only taking-off at the bottom of the wave. This also meant some pretty heavy wipeouts!

Rebecca was unconsciously searching for a balance, not taking off too early (her original mistake) nor too late (overcorrecting). After many wipeouts – and this is where persistence and a positive attitude has a major role – she achieved the balance she was looking for. She took off at the right moment, dropped-in on the wave and then impressed everyone with a spectacular carve at the bottom of the wave (she had to be a snowboarder). After her spontaneous bottom turn, she caught the open face of the wave and surfed it until the end!

Rebecca's case illustrates the natural difficulty of finding the perfect take-off timing. Finding the precise moment to take off on a wave represents the beginning of the surfing experience and the attaining of "the feeling," which is what this chapter is all about.

The determination needed to achieve "the feeling" is always worthwhile. Even for pros and experienced surfers "going back" to appreciate their take-off and "sliding" across waves is a thrill.[13] The simplest form of surfing, catching a wave, riding it and feeling yourself glide over liquid

---

[13] This thrill after many years of surfing experience is achieved by switching one's stance (i.e., a goofy take-off as a regular foot or a regular foot taking off as a goofy). Try it one day!

emerald, is a truly intense and natural sensation. Every time we catch and flow with a wave, we are in touch with nature's magic. Surfers should never forget the simple magic at the core of their act.

Surf Academy Tip: *Paddling, paddle-turning, duck diving and taking off are techniques that, to be more quickly assimilated, require good fitness levels. Swimming is the most conventional cross-training sport to improve these fitness levels.*

Conclusion

It's easy to understand why the first surfing lessons are an overload for people who have never seen the ocean or a surfboard in their lives. Beginners can be overcome by a frustration that feeds on a true lack of ability and control in the water.

But the truth is that whether the waves are in California, Florida, Australia, Indonesia, Peru, Hawaii, Brazil, Portugal, France or anywhere else in the world, they are all part of a superior force of nature that transcends all human life and knows no justice or injustice, good or evil. The ocean and its waves are unbridled energy. In order to flow and interact with this superior force, surfers need to go through an initiation that will teach them a variety of complex techniques.

It is this initial knowledge of a) observing the waves and ocean conditions; b) understanding the basic measurements of surfboards; c) following wave etiquette; d) respecting and defending nature in the ocean but also in all its forms; e) learning to paddle, paddle-turn, duck dive, and take off that this chapter focused on.

Surfing values such as balance, humility, respect and persistence result in life lessons that are useful during a person's entire lifecycle, from birth to death.

Surfers acquire most of their essential values and attitudes from waves and the ocean, as well as beliefs and understandings that will stay with them for as long as they want to keep learning, creating and evolving not only as surfers but also as human beings.

Old sage experiencing "the feeling" at Rocky Point. The sensation of being in harmony with nature is useful during the surfer's whole life.

Chapter 4

Kelly Slater: riding inside the wave – in the barrel, with commitment and bravado – is surfing's ultimate move.

Photo: Quiksilver

Learning and Developing the 7

Learning *the 7* and investing in surfing technical refinement is only really useful after understanding and enduring Phase 1 (Introduction to the Ocean and Waves):

1) knowing how to **assess and evaluate the surf conditions in different breaks**
2) understanding the basics about **surfboard measurements and dimensions**
3) understanding wave etiquette and respect for other surfers in the water
4) mastering the duck dive and paddling techniques
5) executing the take-off correctly

The theoretical and practical information from Phase 1 will continue to be very important for the developing surfer, especially the fundamentals related to wave and surfboard knowledge. Waves break in all kinds of different sizes and work with different winds, tides and conditions. Wave variety is infinite – no wave is the same. They all have their individual differences. Experienced surfers learn to observe specific kinds of waves, like beachbreaks[14], pointbreaks[15] and reefbreaks,[16] and understand these different waves. As a result, they learn to adapt and specialize their surfing to the different kinds of waves.

This gives rise to a certain cult and veneration towards wave formation and creation – waves are, many times, born thousands of miles from where they will break. When the wind imposes its energy on the great oceans, its continuous speed and pressure on the ocean surface, creates initial ripples which then increase in size and become waves.

The energy that crosses oceans and causes waves is called "swell." Picture trains of organized waves, traveling with more or less constant rhythms and speeds, crossing oceans until they reach your favorite spot. So the next time you catch a wave, try to remember that you were riding and being part of the last glorious and breaking moments of a traveling wave. You are literally feeling the wave. Words are simply insufficient to describe this feeling, one has to go out and try it!

In a different sense, the wave cult is also applied to the surfer's cult of surfboards – the fundamental tool to ride waves. The diversity of existing shapes and materials, the continuous developments in shaping, the aura that surrounds master shapers, the quantity of measurements associated with basic surfboard dimensions and the time and importance given to fine-tuning surfboards make any serious surfer naturally curious and eager to learn about surfboard fundamentals and what works for his/her surfing.

Surf Academy Tip: *Check out wave/swell prediction websites like surfline.com;, windguru.com and fnmoc.navy.mil to understand more about wave formation and swell movements. BUT always use your local break as a reference to compare the predictions. Nothing beats checking the conditions yourself.*

14, 15, 16 See Glossary.

The theoretical and practical elements of Phase 1 give a surfer lifelong knowledge; yet surfing, like learning is a continuous mission. Learning about surfing, deepening one's knowledge regarding wave predictions and different breaks, and surf etiquette, as well as increasing surfboard know-how are the steps that accompany the practicing, learnning and understanding of advanced moves.

The 7 is about learning **seven** very important and advanced moves:

1) **S turns**
2) **Bottom turns**
3) **Roundhouse cutbacks**
4) **Floaters**
5) **Snaps**
6) **Aerials**
7) **Barrels**

The barrel - the move that distinguishes surfing from all other sports.

To execute these moves means mastering the most technical aspects of surfing. This means that the learning of advanced surfing technique is a difficult and lengthy process that demands persistence and dedication. Specifically, it means: 1) surfing regularly, 2) surfing all kinds of ocean conditions and all kinds of different surf breaks, 3) experimenting and adapting surfboards to your surfing and different waves, 4) paying close attention to technique by studying surf magazine photo sequences, this book's photo sequences and watching surf films repeatedly, 5) having a coach and/or coaching sessions evaluate your technique, create training sessions and drills for you to improve your surfing, 6) participating and understanding surf contest criteria and 7) being willing to be conscious of your own mistakes.

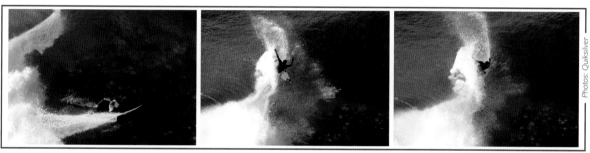

Photos: Quiksilver

The bottom turn is the primordial turn in surfing (see 1ˢᵗ photo) – not only a beautiful move in itself but a move that sets up all quality top-turns (see 2ⁿᵈ and 3ʳᵈ photo).

Francisco had started surfing with his older brothers and cousins before the formation of the Surf Academy's pioneer youth brigade movement, which was led by three young groms: Nicolau, Tomas and Pedro. Francisco wasn't part of the beginning of this group, but he fought hard to be part of it. He surfed a lot during the summer and even surfed big swells, which many of the kids his age would refuse to do.

The problem was that during the winter he didn't surf in a core group of kids like the one described above. For two winters, Francisco was unaware of his group's training sessions. In the summer, he noticed the progress that the others had made and how far behind he was in learning moves. He started to wake up earlier and train harder to deserve his spot in this advanced group. He made substantial progress. Throughout the summer, he was surfing well. He started to regularly make floaters, cutbacks and S turns!

Photo: Quiksilver

The aerial, the most innovative move in surfing. Skateboarding and snowboarding both born from surfing have come to help develop and refine aerial moves in surfing. Grabs, rotations, flips and endless possibilities are being imported and adapted to waves. Dane Reynolds leads the push of endless aerial possibilities.

Francisco is a powerful and competitive junior tennis player. He was brought up in a tennis family, so competing came naturally! So after this great summer of surfing he became totally commited to sustaining his progress in surfing by sticking to the Surf Academy's advanced group throughout the winter.

NOTE: The most common technical mistakes remain if a surfer is unaware of his/her surfing ability, or if he/she doesn't get enough practice throughout the year.

Pedro had trouble generating speed. He was unable to do relaxed, smooth **S turns**. At the time, he couldn't let himself go and relax on the wave – which is essential to achieve speed and flow – so he couldn't consistently generate the speed he needed to perform moves with power and speed. This lack of projection and velocity was reflected in all of Pedro's moves. We worked hard on visualization and on his understanding that he had to be relaxed to generate speed (he is a little bit nervous and stressed on land, so it was actually pretty natural that that would be transferred to the water). It took 3 solid months of working on **S turns** to be able to significantly improve this move.

After experiencing "the feeling," Nicolau (see Chapter 3) went through a very important stage in skill acquisition that allowed him to overcome a problem that had been accumulating since he was a beginner: a two-movement take-off.

This became an interesting case of incomplete practical knowledge acquisition from Phase 1 that influenced learning in Phase 2. Nicolau was losing precious seconds with his two-movement take-off – he used his front knee before actually standing up. This was delaying his first move potential, and it was becoming an increasingly difficult problem to correct. It required intense focus –

through the repetition of correct take-offs in and out of the water – during two months of summer training to eliminate his mistake and prepare him for more complex Phase 2 technical goals.

Nicolau knew that he wanted to continue to improve his surfing; he was already learning the first fundamental moves of *the 7*, S turns, floaters and roundhouse cutbacks, but he would have to go back and train his take-off. This is very tough for a surfer to overcome and train seriously. The importance of drill repetition became, in my understanding, absolutely essential. Nicolau's case of take-off correction perfectly illustrates the difficulties in overcoming certain technical mistakes. Without being too boring we repeated take-off drills in and out of the water until consistent results were obtained – this took almost two months because the problem seemed apparently solved but then it would resurface. Positive results can be claimed only when they are consistent.

NOTE: Frontside and backside distinctions are not made – this means we follow the premise that frontside and backside are mirror, symmetrical movements. The outside rail is symmetrical to the inside rail; toes function as a mirror of the heels. Then front-to-back foot weight transitions; crouch-to-spring leg movements function the same going either way.
This is fundamentally true, but when learning to execute moves, surfers have spontaneous preferences for making certain moves backside and other moves frontside. The mirror seems to have some concave and convex angles!

1 S Turns

DVD: Tito da Costa

Ruben Gonzalez: flow and grace to generate speed in harmony with the wave.

S turns are subtle adjustments from one rail to the other, a rarely identified move. However, they are essential to generating and controlling speed. Velocity must be generated in harmony with the wave. Legs do most of the work, through a crouching-to-release (of legs) spring movement and a rocking from toes-to-heels movement. Velocity should be born in harmony with the wave. Arm movement is minimal: staying stylish yet efficient is what it's all about!

1-2 Use heels to lean on your outside rail, with slight extra weight on the front foot; bend your knees and wind-up your legs like a spring. With minimal arm movement, follow the outside to inside rail transitions.

3 As your legs reach a maximum crouch position, your feet are perfectly centered. Both front and back are almost equally weighted (the back foot always has a slight advantage because of the weight and effect of the fins) and heels and toes are equally weighted.

You are preparing the start of the heels-to-toes, inside-to-outside, crouch to spring, back-to-front foot transition.

4-5 Now pressure is on your toes. Lean on them, pump your inside rail and stretch your legs.

6-8 You have reached your maximum stretch position with maximum weight on the toes. In Frame 7, your inside rail and back foot will be given one last extra push. In Frame 8, you have reached your maximum toes, inside rail and back footweight position. Prepare to keep your balance through the weight transitions (notice how in Frame 6 the surfer is applying more back foot weight and, by Frame 8, he is transferring some of that weight to his front foot).

9 It starts all over again: crouch your legs, put weight on outside rail, on your heels and front foot and prepare to release the "spring" energy in your legs and make the transition to inside rail, toes and back foot.

Once enough speed is generated – depending on the length of a wave's section, about one to three S turn transitions are necessary to generate speed – the surfer should be motionless and glide a little before he enters his next move. You are working to improve your instinct, but don't forget: Once you are up and riding, you have to trust your feeling!

2 Bottom Turns

DVD: Tito da Costa

Teco Padaratz turning hard and continuously at the bottom of the wave.

Bottom turns are the basis of "power surfing." This move consists of a long progressive turn at the bottom or base of the wave. This turn sets up all other moves; it projects the surfer to the most critical and "top" parts of the wave (to execute "top turns" or snaps).

1 You are going down the wave's face, your weight is centered over both feet. You must quickly check what the wave is doing, to anticipate the angle of the wave. The angle of the wave will dictate what your top turn is going to be.

2 You've felt your spot at the bottom of the wave and started your bottom turn looking at your chosen spot at the top of the wave – the spot where you'll execute your "top turn." You are leaning hard on your toes and inside rail, looking exactly at where you are going to turn at the top of the wave. Keep your knees bent, weight centered over both feet (while you are leaning over your toes) intent to keep your speed throughout the turn, because the turn has just started!

3   Keep your eyes set on where you want to go. Stay low, compact, centered and leaning hard on your toes and inside rail.

4   Now you are starting to climb the wave's face. The turn is starting to sharpen. Put slightly more weight on your back foot and no longer lean as hard on your toes.

5   You are in full "climb" mode, power is still on your back foot, the weight on your toes has reached its maximum and is preparing its transition to your heels. You are still focused on your turning spot at the top of the wave – don't stop bottom turning until you've reached the very top!

6   You still haven't reached the top of the wave, but your weight is now centered over your feet and is just about to switch to your heels. Back foot is still powering and your back arm is getting into action to fuel the last stages of your climb up the wave.

7   With the help of your back arm, you are managing to climb with speed right to the top of the wave. Weight is still on your back foot but a transition is starting: your weight is on your heels as you prepare a sharp and radical change of direction. You will feel the speed of your board "hit" a sweet spot at the top of the wave and that is when (and only when) your bottom turn has finished.

8   The back foot power is at its maximum. You are now leaning over your heels and your back arm is fully swung up, your torso and head looking sideways ready to unleash your top turn.

The 7 BOTTOM TURN COACHING TIP:
Bigger waves and bigger boards cause the bottom turn to be more prolongued, so create excellent training conditions for perfecting smooth, continuous bottom turns.

Sudden bursts of progress in advanced surfing do happen, but they never come all at once. André, like Francisco, was a late-comer to our advanced training group, but he was unable to keep up. I remember that after something like two months of training sessions (less than 20 sessions), Andre's parents came to me to discuss their son's progress.

Showing a healthy interest in Andre's training was really positive, but they were also concerned that he should have already learned more moves, already be sponsored and show up in the magazines! I had to explain that that wasn't the purpose of advanced surf training and to properly learn advanced moves and technique and be recognized for that simply takes time.

Parents specifically and everyone in general should be aware that the learning process for *the 7* is slow. There is so much to learn with this method that it has to be taken in gradually.

Photo: Quiksilver

Photo: Carlos Pinto

All surf coaches know that no move is truly well executed without a good bottom turn. This turn can be refined using bigger boards. This forces the surfer to correctly use the rail on the wave (or else the board simply doesn't turn).

It is useful (not essential) for your surf coach to practice what he teaches: João De Macedo practicing.

Photo: AJ Neste/Surfing America

Kelly Slater (previous page) and Tanner Gudauskas (above) show perfect bottom turn positioning – low center of gravity, surfboard on rail, maintaining speed througout the turn and eyes set on where to turn at the top of the wave.

3 Roundhouse Cutback

DVD: Tito Da Costa

Tiago Pires shows perfect rail use and and a strong hit off the whitewater in this textbook roundhouse cutback.

Since this move basically includes two fundamental turns, the cutback and the snap, mastering it means mastering the use of your rail to carve on a wave's open face, which is what power turns are all about. But maintaining speed and sharpness is what finesse is all about. Combining these contradictory forces is what makes the roundhouse cutback one of the most beautiful and complex turns in surfing.

1   Approach this move with a small open face bottom turn

2-3   Start turning/carving off your heels and inside rail. Back foot power allows the start of the turn to be sharp. Back arm stays low and close to your outside rail (grabbing your rail makes it a bit harder to complete the roundhouse, but is also an option) while your front arm shows the way.

4-5   Now you are carving. A slight weight transition has been made to your front foot, and you are starting to look to where you are going. You must look at where you are going (Frame 5) to keep momentum throughout the turn and maintain enough speed to "hit" hard off the whitewater. Your back arm is still just over your outside rail and your front arm has passed from "showing the way" to being a pivot around which the turn is being made. Your goal is to turn continuously and sharply without losing speed or breaking the arc of your turn.

6-7   You are still carving and keeping your weight on your heels while spreading a little more weight towards your front foot (Frame 6). You are looking straight at where you want to turn and are starting to put a little more weight on your back foot to allow yourself to climb and "hit" the whitewater (Frame 7).

8-9   You have stopped looking to where you want to "hit," and are actually "hitting" the whitewater. Bank hard off your back foot, throw your back arm up and turn your torso and head to allow the second move of the roundhouse to be completed (i.e., the whitewater "hit" or snap).

10-12 You are fully compressed in the whitewater and completing your snap. Aim your board for the bottom of the wave. Stretch your legs a little to give yourself a little extra speed (Frame 12) but stay crouched and low to ride out the bumps of the whitewater. You've gone to the most powerful part of the wave. Stay calm and keep your speed for your next move. Prepare to attack the next section.

It is extremely difficult to maintain speed through the cutback and snap moves that make up a roundhouse cutback. That is what makes it so powerful yet radical and smooth, when well executed.

Photo: Aaron Checkwood/BodyGlove

Holly Beck uses her rail to lean hard and turn the board around to get back to the most powerful part of the wave.

Photos: Carlos Pinto

José Gregorio performs a frontside roundhouse cutback. This turn is one of the most complex and difficult moves of the 7. The surfer must have speed, power and the finesse to make subtle weight transitions. All 7 moves can improve a lot by watching good surf films and seeing yourself surfing. The more you progress, the more fun you have.

Photos: Quiksilver

Dane Reynolds' optimum rail control throughout this super fast carve. From Frame 6 onwards, he decides to just push the cutback instead of getting into a roundhouse. Look closely at how Dane's head is not looking at where he is going.

Photos: Quiksilver

Fred Patacchia leans smoothly on his inside rail, maintains his speed and brings it all around, keeping his eyes on where he wants to go to make this turn a roundhouse cutback.

Kalani Robb uses his body and surfboard to generate speed and then powerfully carve his outside rail into this beautiful cutback.

Photos: AJ Neste/Surfing America

The 7 is a working platform upon which surfers can refine their technique. From the moment it is known and well executed, surfers can combine the 7 and create variations that lead to transformations and distortions of the 7: like this "tailsliding cutback."

Tom's *floaters* are one of his weaknesses: he is generally unable to stay gliding on top of the wave for too long. He goes up but then comes straight down. To further the glide on top of the wave, he has to bend his knees more and put slightly more weight on his front foot. So we began with a *floater* drill that focused fundamentally on gliding on top of the lip – ideally landing the move, but gliding on top of the lip was the priority.

Watching a video of Tom's *floater* attempts greatly helped him visualize his mistakes and work to correct them in his next surf session. After achieving more glide we worked on keeping his balance, positioning and momentum on his board when landing – to allow sufficient speed – to efficiently set up his next move. As with Pedro, we had to keep working on this move for 3 solid months before we could consider Tom was executing *floaters* consistently. Fun repetition and persistence applies for all of *the 7*.

4 Floater

Paulo Moura floats and glides to pass over a section.

The floater is a relatively modern move, developed by surfers like Martin Potter, Cheyne Horan and Richie Collins in the 1980s. It involves a totally different form of riding the top of the wave; no longer "top turning." Instead of "top turning," the surfer is floating! This move involves gliding and not turning.

1   Approach the section you want to "float" over with a mid-face bottom turn. Look and aim at where you are going to climb onto the lip.

2   You are on the lip just about to start to float and glide over it. Put weight on your back foot to get the board up and also pull up your arms for extra projection onto the lip. Pass the pressure from your toes and inside rail to a more centered position to allow the board to glide on its bottom (as opposed to its rails). Bend your knees and stay low as you glide.

3   You have successfully climbed onto the lip. Stay crouched and in control of your board. Put a little more pressure on your front foot and heels so that the board's bottom is gliding and you stay on the wave, instead of falling off behind it.

4   You are still floating! To compensate the beginning of your downward motion – from the floating position – stay centered by keeping a little weight on your front foot. You're compensating for the downward motion of the falling lip by putting weight and pressure over your front foot and toes.

5 The slight extra pressure on your front foot and toes is showing its results: you are still floating and traveling along the wave. Notice how the heels of the front foot are not even in contact with the board. This is the floating position: knees bent in a slightly crouched position, board gliding on top of the wave's falling lip and weight on front foot and toes.

6 You are free-falling down with the wave's falling lip. Your legs are stretched because the board has dropped down with the wave. You keep control over your board by keeping your body and feet centered over it. Now you put slightly more weight on your back foot to avoid falling forward over your board.

7-8 Bend your knees and get back to a more crouched position. Stay centered over your board to ride out any bumps. Your eyes are already set on where you want to go and what you want to do next. You use the spring energy in your legs and momentum from your arms for a short, quick bottom turn to project you from your landing into another move.

The floater is more spectacular the longer the surfer stays gliding on top of the lip and the hollower the wave's section the surfer is floating over. But don't underestimate the difficulty of controlling your speed and landing a floater over an apparently mushier whitewater section of a wave. "Don't forget that landing with speed while staying in control by being able to set up and execute another move is a sign of true surfing mastery!"

Photos: Quiksilver

Landing can be difficult if you are going fast and free-falling off the lip. It is essential to stay confident and have strong knees! Kelly Slater (left) and Mick Fanning (right) prepare to land.

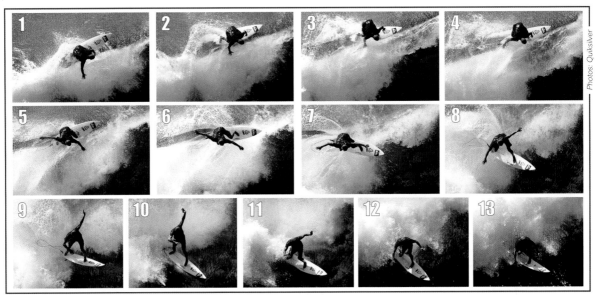

Photos: Quiksilver

Kelly Slater demonstrates a textbook backside projection floater over a long whitewater section. This is even more spectacular when you know this floater was executed in preparation for another move further down the line.

Photos: AJ Neste/Surfing America & Aaron Checkwood/BodyGlove

Karina Petroni and Travis Mellem demonstrate how the floater reentry is a very different kind of floater, because the surfer is no longer landing parallel to beach but instead follows the lip of the breaking wave sideways, aiming his/her board towards shore as the move is completed.

Kelly Slater floating in Nias - notice the board being perfectly parallel to the breaking wave.

5 Snap/Top Turn

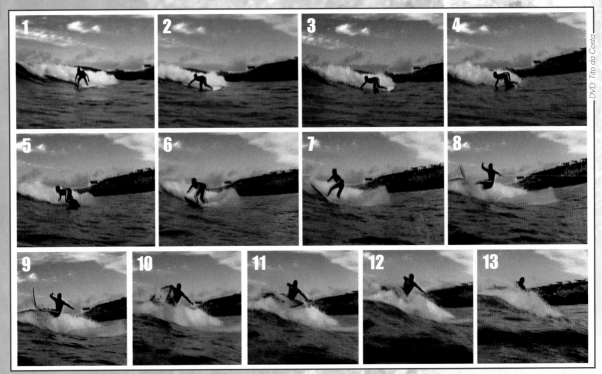

DVD: Tito da Costa

Ruben Gonzalez bottom turns and then turns fast and loose off the whitewater in a classic snap.

The snap/top turn comes in many, many forms. It is a move completely dependent on a good bottom turn and the angle of the top of the wave (depending on how critical the section is, the Top Turn will have to naturally adapt). The subtle weight transitions and arm movements play a crucial role in maintaining and generating speed in this turn.

1-3   You have correctly executed your bottom turn, allowing you to come off the bottom of the wave with speed and aim where you are going to "hit," snap and turn. You leaned hard on your toes and inside rail, passed from a (relatively more) centered stance (Frames 1 and 2) to a position with more pronounced back foot weight.

4-6 Throughout your bottom turn, your eyes are on your target: the place at the top of the wave you want to "hit." To keep upward momentum, the legs are going from a low (Frame 4) to a more stretched position (Frame 6). Simultaneously, the front arm is directing the body and board towards its "target," while the back arm is winding up to get in action.

Release pressure from your toes and inside rail while also applying more back foot power to lift up your board in anticipation of the "hit."

7-8 Your board has hit and is prepared to turn. The weight on your feet is centered between your toes and heels, with back foot pressure still predominate. Your legs are stretched (Frame 7), and you are gradually unwinding your back arm until it is fully up (Frame 8). The momentum of your back arm and making your head, upper body and torso rotate and look sideways will lead the way for your board, legs and hips to follow and keep the move fast and tight. Don't forget: rotate your head, upper body and torso to anticipate (winding/twisting-up effect) the swift rotation of your legs and lower body.

9-11 So now your front foot is fully extended over the board, back foot slightly bent (not visible) and both feet have weight on heels (especially front foot). Your head, arms and upper body are fully twisted, and your back arm is up in anticipation of your board, legs and hips following through to turn the board (Frames 10 and 11).

While turning and "untwisting" the upper body, the weight on your feet is passing from back-foot control to front-foot pressure and direction, loosening the board in the lip and making the turn much faster and radical. By Frame 11, you have turned from going up to coming down in a very tight arc. The turn has been done in a small area at the top of the wave (especially when compared to the area used during a roundhouse cutback, for example).Turn your head to look down over your board's nose to allow yourself to control your descent. The front foot pressure is being released and a more centered stance is adopted to prevent the board from nose diving. Notice how the back arm, the shoulders and the head now have very little movement as you must stay balanced to continue to drop down the wave. You need to maintain your speed and momentum to prepare for your next move.

12-13 Keep control of your descent with balance and minimal body movements. Your weight is centered over both feet, with a little pressure going back to your toes to get the board off its inside rail and on its bottom. Your body is back to a slightly crouched position with arms down, ready to ride out any bumps on the wave and guarantee a successful recovery.

Pushing the move a little further: The same back foot to front foot quick weight transition is applied in the fins free snap, a quasi-aerial top turn; except the weight transitions are pushed a little further, shooting the fins above the lip and out of the wave.

Photos: Quiksilver

The carving backside top turn the turn ends with the board facing the shore yet sometimes the board is pushed even further.

Photos: AJ Neste/Surfing America

Alex Gray and the traditional small wave backside snap. Observe how the fundamental back foot to front foot transition allows the board to loosen up and throw water.

Photos: Quiksilver

The most critical and fast turn in surfing. The surfer must enter the maneuver with a lot of projection from the bottom in order to be able to turn the board at an angle of about 180º, within a very small and vertical space in the wave. The result of a good snap is the most amazing spray of water of all the maneuvers. Again, there are almost endless possible variations to the snap.

Kelly Slater and a textbook snap: perfect torso torsion, quick and sharp back foot power to front foot finesse, and excellent use of the arms for extra projection (Photo 2). You can almost feel the speed he carries coming out of the move.

Kelly Slater shows us a majestic and radical carving top turn. The angle of the wave's face dictates how much carve or snap goes into the turn. The less vertical, the more carves can be put in. Compare both sequences on this page and observe how a more vertical section (top sequence) allows the board (compare Photo 1) to also be more vertical and faster out of the turn (compare Photo 2).

Team USA member Jeremy Johnston demonstrates the 1-2 hit of the snap – a beautiful and fast change of direction. Back-to-front foot transition must be quick and powerful. Speed and balance are essential to allow a fast exit to set up another move down the line.

Clay Marzo pushes his snap over the lip, releasing his fins while maintaining total control.

CJ Hobgood pushes this frontside snap to the limit. Check out his super extended back leg and how his front leg is compressed with almost all weight on his front foot.

Aerial

Photos: Carlos Pinto

Cory Lopez generates speed and then flies high and controlled.

The aerial is the most innovative move in surfing.

1-2 You need speed and momentum when approaching an on-coming section if you want to fly. So, it is crucial to apply at least one or two efficient S turns.

3-5 Use a short, mid-face bottom turn while winding up your arms and legs to get maximum projection from your move. Lean on your toes in usual frontside bottom turn mode and aim for your launching spot.

6   You feel the board softly "hitting" the section you will use to lift off. Apply back foot pressure and prepare to flick weight onto your front foot to execute the traditional skate-inspired "ollie," which will start your flight. Simultaneously, your weight has passed from your toes (mid-face bottom turn) to your heels and back foot. NOTE: The "ollie" is a fundamental skate trick that requires speed and considerable training. A strong back foot down push and then a quick transition to front foot "flick" and pressure is followed through to get the board airborne

7-9   You are already airborne and are about to flick weight onto your front foot to allow the fins to totally release and achieve more height above the lip line. Be careful and make an effort to stay over your surfboard. This means gently transferring some weight now from your heels back to your toes, so that the board straightens out in the air, allowing you to stay over it. You have been flying, in control, over your board for the last three slides, so enjoy it because you can't stay up in the air forever! Your weight after the back foot push will stay over your front foot, and you want it to stay that away until you connect with the wave again.

10   Put some serious weight on your front foot to control and guarantee a radical descent. You are over your board so keep weight centered between toes and heels, assuming a natural tendency of a slight predominance of the heels. You are still flying, but it is time to start preparing for a good place to land.

11   You have finished your freefall; your legs are extended, so you must prepare to get crouched to absorb the impact. Weight is centered over both feet with a slight predominance of front foot and heels to assure forward motion and rail control through the recovery.

12   You are now fully crouched and must keep control by staying low and ready to ride out any bumps. Landing an aerial is always tricky, but you've made it, so don't blow it now by getting distracted and bumped off your board! "Don't forget: it isn't over until you are in control and ahead of the whitewater."

The wave and the board are moving (while the surfer is in the air), so landing an aerial is a difficult task. Experience will help you start predicting which airs are going to be softer and which ones are to be aborted (such as landing on the flats or where the lip is exploding upward), in order to avoid a painful experience that many times leads to injuries. Unfortunately, sticking with impossible and painful landings is an unavoidable part of the learning process.

Photo: AJ Neste/Surfing America

Photo: Tom Carey/Volcom

Team USA member Dave Ward demonstrates how aerials are part of the competition repertoire that has made contests so much more exciting and fun to watch and participate in.

Aerials are a creative move all on their own! Dave Post rotating and demonstrating the endless beauty of flying.

Photo: Quiksilver

Dane Reynolds is busting out airs like this one on a regular basis. This is simply raising the general level of performance around the world! Yet, to be well executed, aerials should be in tune with the wave's flow so that they are spectacular but also smooth.

Photos: Aaron Checkwood/BodyGlove

The "alley-oop" pushed very high by Dion Agius.

DVD: Tito da Costa

David Weare, 360° reverse front side aerial – this South African surfer shows how, even on a small wave, extremely difficult technical maneuvers can be executed. Once again note how the "ollie" is used and then the 180° rotation on the foam, which is fundamental to guaranteeing control and a successful landing.

Photos: Tito de Costa

Shane Beschen – 360° reverse backside aerial – no comments!

Photo: Quiksilver

Clay Marzo goes for a skate/snow-inspired air. It is super important to keep the flow and relationship between the surfing family open and fertile … it helps fuel creativity!

Photo: Quiksilver

Dane Reynolds' radical air may trick the innocent observer into thinking that flying like this and landing are easy. Flying actually is a little easier, but most problems (and injuries) occur on landing.

Nicolau is still only 16 years old, and he has already achieved strong results defeating older surfers in the Open Divisions. He has fantastic speed generated by smooth and efficient *S turns* and a powerful ***bottom-turn*** – progressive and executed right at the bottom of the wave. This allows him to turn in the most vertical upper part of the wave with impressive speed and projection.

Mastering the more complex surfing turns and carves at an early age opened the doors for this young surfer to explore his creativity. In modern surfing, loosely speaking, creativity means style, speed, unpredictable variations of *the 7* and aerials. Once he got the fundamentals down, Nicolau's focus was to start including aerials in his repertoire. Again, drill repetition, without becoming too boring, is the key to acquiring new skills.

Photo: Ricardo Bravo

Some kids at our beach started to try some of Nicolau's aerials, which is good fun but can become a barrier to improvement. "To attempt ***aerials*** without mastering at least 2 or 3 of the basic 7 first – like bottom turns and cutbacks – is wanting a little too much, too soon. Start with the fundamentals and work your way up."

Some of the tools of the modern surfer: many different surfboards, snowboards, and skateboards (not visible). The relationship between these "grandchildren" of surfing has been very fertile and beneficial for the surfing industry as a whole (of which skate and snowboarding are a part) by crossing ideas, ways of being and living as a board rider.

7 Barrels

Photos: Aaron Checkwood/BodyGlove

The no-grab back-side barrel is a ballsy and unpredictable barrel ride executed here perfectly by Bruce Irons at Pipeline.

The barrel is the most intriguing and unique surfing move. Backside barrels are, in principle, more challenging. But developments in equipment has allowed surfers to ride just as deep. Some, like Kelly Slater, Pancho Sullivan, and Bruce and Andy Irons say they can ride even deeper on their backhand at waves like the Pipeline. As with the other *the 7* descriptions, what is important is to imagine yourself executing the move. But in honor of the barrel rider, let's visualize this one through Bruce's movements.

1-2 A correct but risky take-off is absolutely critical for barrel riding. Bruce Irons is known for charging, and these shots illustrate the thickness of the lip and how steep the Pipe drop is. By grabbing the rail, Bruce gains extra control while basically free falling down the wave. Notice he is dropping down on an angle, anticipating the critical trim line necessary for barrel riding.

3 Bruce has made the drop and is now looking for his desired trim line. He shows total bravado by letting go of his rail and resorting only to some tricky footwork to feel out his balance and trim line. He is using his inside rail and weight on his heels to stay away from the liquid guillotine, thus completing his take-off straight into the barrel. Too low on the wave means "being axed"; too high means spinning into the liquid vortex; staying on the desired trim line is easier when you are grabbing your rail, so Bruce is compensating with his left/inner arm directing his board to up the wave face.

4 Having pushed his board up the wave (Photo 3), Bruce is now preparing to compensate and place weight on his outside rail. But this is a transition and almost weightless moment in which he is only slightly using his heels and inside rail while his board is already facing forward anticipating his acceleration (see S turn Move Description).

5 Now staying extra crouched, this is a moment of tension as Bruce presses slightly on his front foot and heels. His board is momentarily directed towards the falling lip to avoid being sucked into the vortex.

6 Still in the barrel, it starts all over again as Bruce sees the oncoming section and needs more speed to make it. Bruce's right (outside) arm is out; he is leaning slightly more on his heels and inside rail, ready to wind up and pump for extra speed.

7 Now less crouched and with his right arm fully out and pushing up, Bruce has used the "spring" energy of his legs and arms to generate more speed in the barrel. Leaning on his heels and inside rail he is following through another S turn.

8 Bruce is now totally pushing his inside rail and his heels, and raising both arms up to bring his board away from the lip and up the wave face away from the falling lip. These are critical S turns: art in motion.

9 Deep in the barrel and completely committed, Bruce has switched his weight slightly away from his heels, putting extra pressure on his front foot dropping down the wave in a repeat action of Photo 4 and 5.

When many would be jumping off their boards, afraid of being caught too deep in the barrel's vortex, Bruce keeps his calm by continuing to accelerate and pump his board. He demonstrates the attitude necessary to make radical and impossible barrels: commitment and faith in the face of difficulty.

Photos: Will Henry

The backside barrel – as much for the surfer, as for the spectator, the barrel represents the most intimate harmony with nature and heightens the technical difficulty of the act to the point that the tube is the sole move in competitive surfing that alone can reach the "perfect" score of 10. Ola Eleogram trains for the score at Rocky Point.

Photos: Quiksilver

Sometimes all you have to do is hang on and keep the faith … still it isn't that easy; inside the barrel, a wipeout is punishing, so keeping your cool is critical!

Photo: Quiksilver

The barrel is the most contradictory and intense maneuver in surfing. Dane Reynolds stalling with his arm and showing calm beyond his years, when many would stress.

CONCLUSION

The 7 is an advanced training method created and developed by the Surf Academy. The method focuses on learning and refining 7 renowned surfing moves to achieve the basis of modern high-performance surfing.

Learning to achieve the necessary concentration to visualize and execute *the 7*[17] will help a surfer improve his/her overall performance on a wave. Repeating drills and moves allows a surfer to understand his/her execution mistakes. This, in turn, allows the surfer to focus on specific problems and not be overwhelmed by his/her technical mistakes. Adopting a systematic

Photo: Quiksilver

Andy Irons charges a massive barrel section. Control and confidence are essential to pull in and then make it out of a barrel. Notice how he uses his inside rail to lean against the wave and his body and arm to stall just as he makes it under the falling lip.

---

[17] The names of the basic surfing maneuvers are debatable and subjective. My aim is to help create a better structure and organization in advanced learning of surfing and not to establish dogmas.

approach to refining technique is essential to improving moves and being consistent, yet maintaining surfing's innate creativity and emotional charge so that achieving consistency is balanced with creativity and performance at the highest level. If surfers don't fall, it means they are not pushing themselves and their performance level is not progressing. Coaches can have a decisive role in helping athletes find and constantly adjust their balance between creativity and consistency.

Once *the 7* are mastered, they can be performed on the same wave to create move combinations: the basis of international high performance. Sequences or move combinations of *the 7* will be the main topic of Chapter 5.

The depth of this method allows for almost infinite technical development. Moves can be endlessly refined and variations creatively invented within *the 7*. Surfing embodies lifetime learning and *the 7* aims to reflect this.

Roundhouse Cutbacks and Floaters

Make sure to bring **how to be a surfer** to the beach to check out the relevant photos and sequences.

Goal:	Execute 3 solid roundhouse cutbacks and 3 "gliding" floaters
Before going in the water:	*Visualization (5 min. max.):* Mentally recreate the movements of a roundhouse cutback and a floater (insist on visualizing the whole move, from set-up to completion).
Drill Overview:	*Water* – Executing roundhouse cutbacks and floaters *Beach* – Physical conditioning.
Duration:	*Water – 1h* = 20 min. each session x 3 *Beach – 20 min* = 5-10 min. each session x 3 *End – 20 min heat*
Drill:	*Follow these guidelines for each session:*
(1)	*Water* – Surfer completes 3 roundhouse cutbacks and 3 floaters successfully *Beach* – 5 push-ups / 10 power-leg jumps.
(2)	*Water* – Surfer completes 2 or more roundhouse cutbacks and 2 or more floaters successfully *Beach* – 10 push-ups / 10 power-leg jumps
(3)	*Water* – Surfer only completes 1 roundhouse cutback and 1 floater successfully *Beach* – Run a 1/4 mile on the beach / 20 push-ups / 20 power-leg jumps
(4)	*Water* – Surfer completes 1 or more roundhouse cutback but no floaters *Beach* – Same as (3)
(5)	*Water* – Surfer does not complete 1 roundhouse cutback or 1 floater successfully *Beach* – Run a 1/4 mile on the beach / 25 push-ups / 25 power-leg jumps
After the Drill:	20 min. heat or evaluation between the athletes – Best scores for waves with roundhouse cutbacks and floaters

After the training session: Find the time to join all the surfers and generically discuss the surfers' competitive goals or the surfers' favorite surfer in a surf movie: "Remember watching Kelly's roundhouse cutback and his floater in *Young Guns II*…wasn't it unreal…that is what you are training for" or "Do these moves in a contest and you'll be passing a lot of heats!" Creating a wider context for the surfer's effort is fundamental for remembering goals, as well as staying focused on accomplishing them.

Surfers who had a success rate of two or more out of three are ready for the next drill: Aerial Drill

Bottom Turns and Snaps

Make sure to bring **how to be a surfer** to the beach to check out the relevant photos and sequences.

Goal:	Execute 3 solid bottom turns and 3 controlled and critical snaps
Before going in the water:	*Visualization (5 min. max.):* Completing one bottom turn and one snap (insist on visualizing the whole move, from set-up to completion).
Drill Overview:	*Water* – bottom turns and snaps *Beach* – Conditioning.
Duration:	*Water – 1h* = 20 min. each session x 3 *Beach – 20 min* = 5-10 min. each session x 3 *End – 20 min heat*
Drill:	*Follow these guidelines for each session:*
(1)	*Water* – Surfer completes 3 bottom turns and 3 snaps successfully *Beach* – 5 push-ups / 10 power-leg jumps.
(2)	*Water* – Surfer completes 2 or more bottom turns and 2 or more snaps successfully *Beach* – 10 push-ups / 10 power-leg jumps
(3)	*Water* – Surfer only completes 1 bottom turn and 1 snap successfully *Beach* – Run a 1/4 mile on the beach / 20 push-ups / 20 power-leg jumps
(4)	*Water* – Surfer completes 1 or more bottom turn but no snaps *Beach* – Same as (3)
(5)	*Water* – Surfer does not complete 1 bottom turn or 1 snap successfully *Beach* – Run a 1/4 mile on the beach / 25 push-ups / 25 power-leg jumps
After the Drill:	20 min. heat between the athletes – Best scores for waves with bottom turns and snaps.

After the training session: At the beach, create a context for discussing the surfer's competitive goals or the surfer's favorite surfer in a surf movie: "Remember watching Kelly's bottom turns and snaps in *Young Guns II*…wasn't it unreal…that is what you are training for" or "Do these moves in a contest and you'll be passing a lot of heats!" Creating a wider context for the surfer's effort is fundamental for remembering goals, as well as staying focused on accomplishing them.

Surfers who had a success rate of two or more out of three are ready for the next drill: Aerial Drill

Aerial

Make sure to bring **how to be a surfer** to the beach to check out the relevant photos and sequences.

Goal:	Execute 3 solid and controlled aerials
Before going in the water:	*Visualization (5 min. max.):* Completing a controlled and high areal (insist on visualizing the whole move, from set-up to completion).
Drill Overview:	*Water –* Aerials *Beach –* Conditioning
Duration:	*Water – 1 h* = 20 min each session x 3 *Beach – 20 min* = 5-7 min. each session x 3 *End – 20 min heat*
Drill	*Follow these guidelines for each session:*
(1)	*Water –* Surfer completes 3 aerials successfully *Beach –* 5 push-ups / 10 power-leg jumps.
(2)	*Water –* Surfer completes 2 or more aerials successfully *Beach –* 10 push-ups / 10 power-leg jumps
(3)	*Water –* Surfer only completes 1 aerial successfully *Beach –* Run a 1/4 mile on the beach / 20 push-ups / 20 power-leg jumps
(4)	*Water –* Surfer does not complete 1 aerial successfully *Beach –* Run a 1/4 mile on the beach / 25 push-ups / 25 power-leg jumps
After the Drill:	20 min. heat between the athletes – Best scores for waves with aerials.

After the training session: At the beach, create a context for discussing the surfer's competitive goals or the surfer's favorite surfer in a surf movie: "Remember watching Craike's aerials in *Young Guns II*…wasn't it unreal…that is what you are training for" or "Complete your aerials in a contest and you'll be passing some heats and earning some serious prize money!" Creating a wider context for the surfer's effort is fundamental for remembering goals, as well as staying focused on accomplishing them.

Surfers who had a success rate of two or more out of three are ready for the next drill: Roundhouse Cutbacks and Floaters

S-Turns and Barrels

Make sure to bring **how to be a surfer** to the beach to check out the relevant photos and sequences.

Goal:	Execute 2 backside and 2 frontside barrels with pumping S turns before tucking under the curl.
Before going in the water:	*Visualization (5 min. max.):* "Pumping in the barrel," executing S turns in the barrel or just before getting under the curl (insist on visualizing the whole move, from set-up to completion).
Drill Overview:	*Water* – S-Turns and barrels *Beach* – Conditioning
Duration:	*Water – 1 h 30 min* = 30 min. each session x 3 *Beach – 15/20 min* = 5/7 min. each session x 3 *End – 30 min heat*
Drill	*Follow these guidelines for each sessions:*
(1)	*Water* – Surfer completes 2 waves with tight in the pocket or in the barrel S turns *Beach* – 5 push-ups / 10 power-leg jumps
(2)	*Water* – Surfer only completes 1 wave with tight in the pocket or in the barrel S turns *Beach* – Same as (1)
(3)	*Water* – Surfer does not complete 1 barrel or tight under the curl S turns successfully *Beach* – 15 push-ups / 15 power-leg jumps
After the Drill:	20 min. heat between the athletes – Best scores for waves with S-Turns and Barrels.

After the training session: Create a context for discussing the surfer's competitive goals or the surfer's favorite surfer in a surf movie: "Remember watching Brooko's, Kelly's or Dane's backside pumping barrel in *Young Guns II*…wasn't it unreal…how about Dane's pumping backside in the barrel, then coming out grabbing the rail…that is what you are training for" or "Take off deep and pump hard. You'll be amazed with what you'll pull off in a contest. You'll be passing a lot of heats, when the waves are barreling!" Creating a wider context for the surfer's effort is fundamental for remembering goals, as well as staying focused on accomplishing them.

Surfers who had a success rate of two or more out of three are ready for the next drill: Aerial Drill.

Note: Conditions must cooperate to successfully execute this drill.

Chapter 5

Famous waves, like for example, Jeffrey's Bay in South Africa (above), Bells Beach in Australia, and Trestles in California, are renowned for being so perfect. High performance on these waves involves making and connecting multiple moves.

Being a Surfing Athlete – Creatively Combining the 7

After learning the theory and executing each of the moves that make up *the 7*, we can go on to an even more advanced stage: executing combinations of *the 7* on the same wave.

This is an elite level of surfing. Managing to execute *the 7* in various combinations or sequences without losing speed or flow is pure surfing magic! It is a stage of development reserved for only an elite number of surfers in the world. Combining various well-executed moves on one wave requires precise technique, instinct and balance to allow momentum and speed between moves. Finding surfers who have reached the level necessary to do this kind of more advanced technical training is rare.

DVD: Tito da Costa

Ruben Gonzalez perfectly combining S turns and a bottom turn: the most basic combination of the 7. Keeping control of the board with minimal body movements along all these weight adjustments is what shows a surfer's style and skill.

Examples of Combinations of *the 7*:

1) **S turns – Bottom Turn**
2) **Bottom – Snap, Cutback or Air + Bottom – Snap, Cutback or Air (double move combo)**
3) **Floater – Snap (at the most vertical part of the wave)**
4) **Roundhouse – Snap**
5) **S turns – Barrels**
6) **Snap – Air**
7) **Barrel – Air or Roundhouse Cutback**

Photo: Will Henry

A good surfer must learn to ride and rip all kinds of waves and difficult conditions. Yet long and perfect waves like this left-hand pointbreak in California allow multiple moves, which means they are the best training ground for practicing combinations of the 7.

Today, Nicolau is a world tour hopeful. We started training many years ago. He and his group of young groms were some of the Surf Academy's first students. After more than four years training, he has continued to evolve. Recently I mentioned to him that his roundhouse cutback had improved greatly but challenged him to combine – with flow – this move and properly set up a snap.

When talking to him about it, I made him visualize a roundhouse cutback as part of a combination or sequence of moves executed on the same wave. After completing the roundhouse, he had to have speed and flow to come off the bottom of the wave and complete a snap *(see digital sequences)*. The biggest challenge of all combinations of *the 7* is to maintain speed and momentum from one move to another.

Santa Cruz right-hand point break in all its glory. Don't be spoiled to think you learn to surf in perfect and long waves. Taking full advantage of these conditions really only comes when the surfer demonstrates individual control of at least five of the 7. Then training and "putting it all together" makes all the more sense.

The important issue for a talented surfer, like Nicolau, Tomas, Pedro or Francisco, is finding specific areas for improvement. This allows the surfer and coach to pinpoint weaknesses or areas of improvement instead of getting lost in a multiplicity of advanced surfing objectives. But at this level of surfing, improvements are less obvious and generally take long to achieve. My challenge as a coach is to keep these surfers motivated so that they continue to work hard on their specific goals. For Nicolau it meant not losing focus of his roundhouse-snap objective.

Photo: AJ Neste/Surfing America

Taking your flag up on the podium is always a buzz and a great honor.

In order to execute combinations of *the 7* without losing the wave's potential, the surfer must be able to visualize the combination of moves in his mind before going out to surf and then execute the combination in the water.

On the wave there is no time to think; the moves must come out instinctively so what the coach and the surfer are working on is the sharpening of the instinct.

Eddie is another interesting case of the natural difficulty in learning new move combinations on a wave. He is a talented and an increasingly famous junior surfer like Nicolau, yet, after watching him surf, I encouraged him to try out a *floater-snap* sequence. We drove an hour and half to a well-known left-hand pointbreak where he could more easily train this sequence (see page 125).

DVD: Tito da Costa

Ben Bourgeois performing the floater-snap combination. After landing the floater with control and speed, when the surfer is at the bottom of the wave, he does a solid and continuous bottom turn, projecting himself upwards onto the lip. Coordination and maintenance of speed are essential skills for completing combinations of the 7.

Surf Academy's Tip: *Move combinations represent the highest and most technical level of surfing since radicalness and flow are ideally combined to create these sequences. To reach this level, watch a lot of surf films but when watching search for specific combinations, for example, a floater-snap combination that you can then include and repeat in your training sessions.*

DVD: Tito da Costa

Roundhouse-snap/top turn: this combination demands extreme coordination, balance and flawless rail-to-rail transitions. The roundhouse cutback is executed with continuous rail drive. Coming off the whitewater is where most problems occur. Driving through the whitewater's bumps, the legs work as springs that absorb impact and maintain speed. The surfer must maintain enough speed to execute a strong bottom turn that will allow the momentum for a hard snap and the success of the combination. Tiago Pires demonstrates how it's done. Look closely at the transitions from roundhouse to snap in the frames.

USA Surf Team Head Coach Peter Townend gives encouragement to Karina Petroni after a difficult heat. Keeping athletes confident and focused is one of the coach's major roles.

The visualization and execution of this sequence is completely different from the usual *bottom turn-snap* combination. It is important for the surfer to be in the middle of the wave to prepare a long floater. Usually the surfer takes off sideways and stays in the middle of the wave doing *S turns* until *floating* onto the lip. After passing over the section and completing the *floater,* the surfer lands at the bottom of wave with enough control and speed to allow him to set up for a good *bottom turn,* which will project him into a *snap*.

Eddie was having a lot of trouble not doing *bottom turns* immediately after the take-off. He was not used to generating enough speed to float over long sections and through a solid bottom turn to, prepare his snap. Therefore, Eddie was losing the wave's full potential by going straight for a *bottom turn-snap* combination instead of floating over certain sections to then make the whole wave and perform more moves on it.

Group spirit of the teams is different than the individual spirit of the athlete competitor. Despite this distinction, companionship is still felt even in the most individual and competitive professional circuits.

DVD: Tito da Costa

Barrel + roundhouse – at the exit of the barrel, the speed and adrenalin level is such that the surfer's concentration must increase to overcome those sensations in order to execute a completely different maneuver.

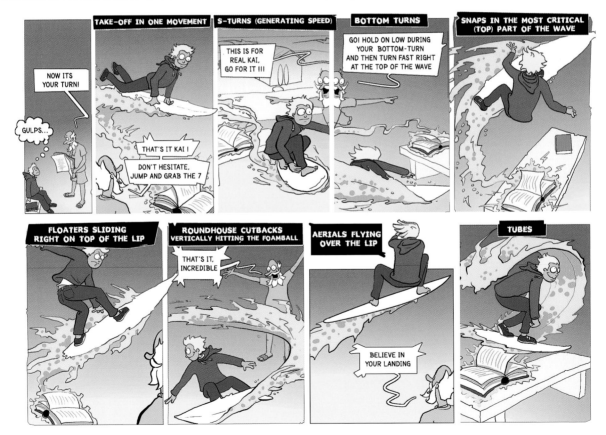

This type of more advanced technical training demands the help of a video camera. The video camera is a great tool to perfect techniques. Athletes generally enjoy and have fun analyzing their waves on film. This fact reinforces the positive benefits of using a video camera as an essential surf coaching tool. Seeing and recognizing a mistake is the first step towards correcting it. And if you can have fun learning how to correct it, that's even better!

Tony "the Tiger" is a radical surfer. He is a hot under-21 – another world tour hopeful. He likes to include radical maneuvers in his repertoire: aerials, 360° reverses, 360° floaters, and ally-oops. He usually sacrifices a whole wave to make just one move – but what a move it is!

DVD: Tito da Costa

Florida's Cory Lopez demonstrates a snap/top turn + aerial sequence: after completing the snap, the surfer generates speed to be able to take off and fly over the lip.

Tony Dias is another surfer, quite different from Tony "the Tiger". "Smooth Tony" as we call him, likes to connect moves as effortlessly as possible. He is always trying to maximize the wave's potential by creating different move combinations on his waves and using the wave's full length. He always looks for a wave with a potential to do at least two or three moves. This sometimes makes his surfing a little too predictable.

Both these surfers have a lot to learn from each other. "Radical Tony" has to smooth out his style, make more moves on each wave and try to cool down his speed "wiggles" when obsessively searching for ramps on his waves. "Smooth Tony" has to get a bit more amped on the wave and try experimenting more with aerials and fin-free/sliding surfing. To execute combinations of *the 7* (especially ones including aerial moves like an aerial-snap combination), demands a lot, even from the best. But it goes to show that even today radical surfing isn't

Photo: Carlos Pinto

Complementary training and physical preparation can be very important for surfers who wish to work on improving their surfing and achieve higher levels of consistency. The work in the pool and the gym never substitutes (nor can reduce) training in the ocean, but it can certainly help to measure effort and the will of the athlete to progress and win. Effort and a strong will are fundamental qualities for consistent success in competition and big waves.

everything, so when a radical move is executed with speed and flow, allowing the surfer to prepare still another move down the line, then you know you are witnessing a freak surfer going off!

Thinking about these two surfers' different approaches to riding waves underlines how difficult and subtle it is to keep talented surfers on the road to continual improvement. Combining both flow and radical styles requires a lot of concentration and effort for body and mind to be able to solve the apparent "smooth" – "radical" contradiction. Nowadays to be a professional surfer requires this combination of radicalness and flow on a wave. This fact makes high-performance extremely creative, diverse and unpredictable.

Young surfers' gradual search for balance and development will certainly bear fruit if there is enough determination and discipline. The typical teenage and young adult distractions make it harder to focus and be persistent. That is why so few make it. Coaches have a big role in explaining certain sacrifices that come with being a pro: surfers must understand the weight of maintaining certain habits and how consistently choosing the "go out; hang out and party" option has long-term, negative consequences. Without moralizing their athletes, coaches

DVD: Tito da Costa

Snap/top turn + aerial – the magic of move combinations, in the words of Rob Machado, resides in the movements and the reading of the wave between the maneuvers. Sometimes it's necessary, for example, to use S turns to pass sections to then find a part of the wave to perform an unpredictable big radical move or a different move combination.

can greatly help to create a junior athlete's growth path. This support contributes to the longevity of a surfing career and to avoid the always impending "burn-out." Having fun and cutting loose is very important for surfers' creativity and spontaneity, but to be a pro is more than just having fun. Understanding the benefits of cross training and physical preparation can help athletes gain more strength, both physically and mentally. Especially for competitors the hard work ethic behind physical preparation contributes to maintaining confidence and "hunger" for winning.

Physical Preparation and Conditioning

Surfers who have reached and maintained an international level of performance surfing have had to "pay their dues." That means effort and dedication are fundamental parts of achieving success. Today, that is often translated into following some kind of complementary physical preparation program. Even the most talented surfers have to make an effort to keep their edge.

Physical conditioning and other forms of cross-training can be very important parts of the coaching scheme of an advanced surfer athlete. It can help to develop the surfer's maximum potential and physical capabilities. Every surfer has strengths and weaknesses that must be worked on, especially once a very high level of surfing and performance has been achieved.

There are *two* fundamental kinds of physical conditioning:
1) *GENERAL*, which is directed at the development of physical capacities and a harmonious growth

of all areas of the body, without any specific physical requirements. Sports and activities, such as swimming, biking, running, playing soccer, basketball, etc., are all GENERAL forms of physical conditioning; and 2) *SPECIFIC*, which is related to the development of the qualities and habits that are specific to the sport. Both GENERAL and SPECIFIC physical conditioning must be adapted to the surfer's age, surfing ability, training preferences, frame of mind and well-being throughout the training process.

Regarding general and specific surf training, we recommend using an array of sources for preparation, i.e.: gym, pool, yoga, and beach training, which then require specific drills and exercises to improve certain individual weaknesses, such as leg power, paddling power, underwater resistance, etc.

Establishing objectives is a fundamental part of organizing a training scheme. Talking to your coach or a professional personal trainer is helpful to develop some exercises to work on. We have included some physical conditioning exercises in our technical surf drills to underline the importance of fine tuning one's body.

Therefore, there will be specific times to develop the body's general surfing motor skills and power (strength, resistance, speed and flexibility), as well as refining the body's balance skills. Both general and balance exercises work in different ways to strengthen the bodywork in different ways to strengthen the body, which helps minimize injuries and exhaustion. Finally, physical preparation must work to avoid excessive early-age specialization and burn-out. Up-and-coming professional athletes must be adults and balanced human beings, not exclusively contest winning machines. This is difficult to follow and put into practice in very competitive environments. Judging has a very important role because surfing has such an important artistic and creative component that must be valued by judges to allow more creative and spontaneous surfers to win heats and contests. Surfing, through the example of its athletes, can also help other sports be more creative and performance-based instead of excessively tactical and risky. Understanding the benefits of cross-training and physical preparation can help talented athletes gain more strength, both physically and mentally. Especially for competitors, the hard work ethic behind physical preparation contributes to maintain confidence and the "hunger" for winning.

Warm-up (left photo) before and stretch before and after surfing (right photo).

Warm-up before, Stretching after Surfing

A good warm-up is adapted to the training or competition conditions (size of surf, kind of wave, duration of surf), to the environment (air temperature, water temperature, humidity, etc.) and finally to the surfer's personal characteristics and preferences. The body's main systems should be stimulated (blood, breathing, muscle and nervous systems) in a gradual form so as to avoid fatigue and loss of energy reserves.

There are two stages in which warm-ups are executed: the passive phase, in which the warm-up is inactive (i.e., using a blanket or car heater to warm-up); and the active phase, which is generally considered more efficient and results from the surfer's activity. We'll focus on stretching exercises that are more useful after surfing. They can be used as a quick stretch to help concentrate and focus before a surf, but we recommend a quick running/jumping warm-up. These four active warm-up principles are the basics:

1) Running or Jumping
2) Stretching
3) General Mobilization
4) Breathing Exercises

Photo: Carlos Pinto

1 *Running or Jumping – promotes the increase of muscular temperature and breathing rate, and stimulates the nervous system.*

Photo: Carlos Pinto

2 *Stretching – done before and after a session (free surf and competition) in order to relax the mind and regulate the body. By reducing muscular tension, coordination improves because flexibility increases, as does the body`s range of motion (i.e., more radical maneuvers). In preventing accidents, such as pulled muscles, streching develops bodily consiousness, activates circulation and helps release movements blocked by emotional tension. A good stretch should last at least 10 minutes.*

Photo: Carlos Pinto

3 *General Mobilization – exercises done before a surf that stimulate joints (neck, shoulders, elbows, wrists, waist, knees, ankles) and prepare them for a whole range of maneuvers, from snaps to aerials.*

Photo: Carlos Pinto

4 *Breathing Exercises – useful for athletes who are feeling anxiety, fear, nervousness, or lack of confidence, as well as for athletes who are acting apathetic or lethargic before competition.*

Stretching Exercises

Stretching for **the neck**. In the position of a correct posture, straight back and relaxed shoulders, slowly rotate the head, making a complete circle; rotate to the sides; flex and extend the neck forward (neck in contact with the chest) and behind.

Stretching for the *upper portion of the spine and backside of the neck*. This reduces the tension on the neck area, allowing freer movements of the head and neck. Interlacing the fingers behind the head and neck and using the force of the arms, smoothly bring the head forward until feeling a smooth stretching of the *backside of the neck*.

Simple stretching of the *triceps and upper part of the shoulder*. Using the stretched arms over the head, hold the elbow of one of the arms with the other hand and push the elbow gradually behind the head. The movement should be made slowly. Do for both sides.

Stretching of the arms, *shoulders and lateral walls*. This can be done with one arm at a time or with both at the same time, legs flexed, back straight.

Stretching is helpful in keeping the spine relaxed and the body free. With the back totally straight on the floor, bring one leg to the chest keeping the other stretched and the back part of the head bent down. Do for both sides.

131

Stretching *of the thighs*. Support the forearms with the head laid over the hands. Bend one leg forward, perpendicular to the ground, and stretch the other leg behind, with the ankle supported over the ground. Do for both sides.

Stretching of the *quadriceps muscles*. Put one leg forward until the knee of the front leg is exactly on top of the ankle of the same leg, with the other knee supported on the ground. Without moving the foot that is in front, lower the *quadriceps* until feeling a smooth stretch. Do for both sides. Do for both sides.

Cocker position stretches the interior part of the legs, knees, back, ankles, *Achilles tendon and inner tendons*. The legs should be supported on the floor and the fingers pointed outwards at an angle of approximately 15°. The ankles should be 10 to 30 cm apart.

Stretching of the *lumbar region*. Interlace the fingers on the *backside of the neck*, lay the arms on the floor and initiate the stretching of the flexed legs normally. Place a leg over the other so that the supported leg pushes the other in the direction of the floor. Do for both sides.

Stretching for *the thoracic box muscles, abdominals, spine*, shoulders, arms, ankles, and feet. Complete extension of the two arms and two legs with the hands and feet stretched in opposite directions. Stay 5 seconds in this posture and then relax.

Consistency in the quality and quantity of moves is only possible when the surfer's body and mind are perfectly balanced. Achieving individual perfection and harmony between mind and body is an ancient sports ideal and a fundamental part of the underlining goals of all professional surfing athletes. To achieve his/her personal best frequently, the athlete should make an effort at simple things like waking up early, working on a cross-training program and honestly trying his/her hardest to continually progress and improve his technique and results. "No one said it would be easy."

CONCLUSION

Combinations or sequences of *the 7* benefit a lot from visualization and from a surfer's better physical condition. At an advanced level of surfing ability, it has proven very useful to refine advanced techniques through video observation and to follow complementary cross-training programs.

Yet, the most important element for a high-performance surfer is feeling good, strong and confident about oneself. An improvement in the surfer's execution of *the 7*, his or her endurance and consistency when surfing long waves (more than 4 or 5 *the 7 sequences* on the same wave) and his or her ability to complete extreme, apparently impossible moves will directly affect the surfer's performance in the water.

Physical conditioning in regards to video and mental training is generally regarded as being more boring. So making these programs fun is important for surf coaches to be concerned with. Although surfing is such a creative and emotional sport, physical training is also important because it helps the body to be stronger and tends to help the athlete strengthen his/ her mind and feel confident in his/her technical ability and skill. Since there is very little space and time between move combinations, each unnecessary rail movement is potentially fatal for keeping the speed and flow (between moves) on a wave. Confidence, flexibility and strength are essential to good surfing.

Surfing (and being an athlete) at an international competitive level means leading a life that requires some sacrifices. Then the rewards and genuine happiness of achieving our best and doing what we love will make it all worthwhile.

Roundhouse Cutback – Snap Combination

Make sure to bring **how to be a surfer** to the beach to check out the relevant photos and sequences.

Goal:	Train connecting roundhouse cutbacks and snaps on the same wave.
Before going in the water:	*Visualization (5 min max.):* visualize executing and completing a roundhouse cutback-snap combination. "Feel" the connection between moves, the turn, the speed, the surfboard's rails from start to finish of the combination
Drill Overview:	*Water* – Surf 2 waves in a 20 minute session with a roundhouse cutback-snap combination *Beach* – Physical conditioning
Duration:	*Water* – 1 h = 20 min each session x 3 *Beach* – 20 min = 5 min each session x 4 *End* – 30 min heat
Drill: (1)	*Follow these guidelines:* *Water* – Surfer completes 2 or more roundhouse cutback-snap combinations successfully *Beach* – 10 push-ups / 10 power-leg jumps
(2)	*Water* – Surfer completes 1 roundhouse cutback-snap combination successfully *Beach* – 10 push-ups / 10 power-leg jumps
(3)	*Water* – Surfer does not complete 1 roundhouse cutback-snap combination successfully *Beach* – Run a 1/4 mile on the beach / 25 push-ups / 25 power-leg jumps
After the Drill:	30-min heat between the athletes – Best scores for waves with roundhouse-snap combinations

After the training session: Create a context for discussing the surfer's competitive goals or the surfer's favorite surfer in a surf movie: "Remember watching Troy Brooks connecting his moves in *Young Guns II*…wasn't it unreal how after making a roundhouse cutback, he was balanced and in the right spot of the wave to go straight into a Bottom Turn to set up a Snap. That kind of connection between moves is what you are training for!" Creating a wider context for the surfer's effort is fundamental for remembering goals as well as staying focused on accomplishing them.

Surfers who had a success rate of two or more out of three are ready for a different drill: floater-snap combination

Floater-Snap Combination

Make sure to bring **how to be a surfer** to the beach to check out the relevant photos and sequences.

Goal:	Execute and complete floater-snap combinations.
Before going in the water:	*Visualization (5 min. max.):* Executing and completing a floater-snap combination. "Feel" the flow and connection between moves, the speed gliding over the lip, the landing, the bottom turn through turbulence, the speed and precision of the snap: the combination of moves from start to finish.
Drill Overview:	*Water* – Surf two or more waves in a 20-minute session with two distinct floater-snap combinations. *Beach* – Physical conditioning
Duration:	*Water* – 1h = 20 min. each session x 3 *Beach* – 20 min = 5-10 min. each session x 4 *End* – 30 min Heat
Drill	*Follow these guidelines:*
(1)	*Water* – Surfer completes 2 or more floater-snap combinations successfully *Beach* – 10 push-ups / 10 power-leg jumps
(2)	*Water* – Surfer completes 1 floater-snap combination successfully *Beach* – 10 push-ups / 10 power-leg jumps
(3)	*Water* – Surfer does not complete 1 floater-snap combination successfully *Beach* – Run a 1/4 mile on the beach / 25 push-ups / 25 power-leg jumps
After the Drill:	20-min heat between the athletes – Best scores for waves with floater-snap combinations.

After the training session: Create a context for discussing the surfer's competitive goals or the surfer's favorite surfer in a surf movie: "Remember watching Dane connecting his moves in *Young Guns II*...wasn't it unreal how after landing a difficult floater, he would find a spot on the wave and go straight into a Bottom-Turn to set up a Snap Combination. That is what you are training for!" Creating a wider context for the surfer's effort is fundamental for remembering goals as well as staying focused through time on accomplishing them.

Surfers who had a success rate two or more out of three are ready for train the next Drill: double bottom turn-double snap combination

Double Bottom Turn – Double Snap Combination
(i.e., Bottom Turn – Snap + Bottom Turn – Snap)

Make sure to bring **how to be a surfer** to the beach to check out the relevant photos and sequences.

Goal:	Execute two bottom turns and two snaps in a row on the same wave (i.e., a double bottom turn – double snap combination)
Before going in the water:	*Visualization (5 min max.):* Executing and completing a double bottom turn – double snap combination. "Feel" the connection between moves, the speed coming out of the top turns, the bottom turns through turbulence, the surfboard's rails between moves: the moves from start to finish of the combination
Drill Overview:	*Water* – Surf 2 waves in a 20-minute session with a double bottom turn – double snap combination *Beach* – Physical conditioning
Duration:	*Water* – 1 h = 20 minutes each session x 3 *Beach* – 20 min = 5 min each session x 4 *End* – 30 min heat
Drill	*Follow these guidelines:*
(1)	*Water* – Surfer completes 2 or more double bottom turn – double snap combinations successfully *Beach* – 10 push-ups / 10 power- leg jumps
(2)	*Water* – Surfer completes 1 bottom-turn – double snap combination successfully *Beach* – 20 push-ups / 20 power-leg jumps
(3)	*Water* – Surfer does not complete 1 bottom turn – double snap combination successfully *Beach* – Run a 1/4 mile on the beach / 25 push-ups / 25 power-leg jumps
After the Drill:	30 min. heat between the athletes – Best scores for waves with a double bottom-turn – double snap combination

After the training session: Create a context for discussing the surfer's competitive goals or the surfer's favorite surfer in a surf movie: "Remember watching Clay Marzo connecting two ultra radical snaps in *Young Guns II*…wasn't it unreal how after making one ultra critical snap, he was balanced enough to back it up again by nailing a solid bottom turn to set up his second snap. That kind of connection between moves is what you are training for!" Creating a wider context for the surfer's effort is fundamental for remembering goals as well as staying focused on accomplishing them.

Surfers who had a success rate two or more out of three are ready for the next drill: Aerial Drill

Chapter 6

Photo: Quiksilver

Troy Brooks' confident no-grab backside barrel during competition at the Quiksilver Pro-Fiji

Competition Surfing

There have been huge developments in societies and in sports since the start of peaceful and non-violent competitions in ancient Greece. Today's modern era of global high-performance professional competitions, is a far-cry from the original Greek Olympic Games, but certain fundamental values have – and should – endure.

The wisdom and values that support competition point to the importance of accepting and understanding the responsibility of making an effort and always trying to perform at one's best as the essence of being a professional athlete. To fulfill this responsibility, understanding the history and the context of ancient sport and performance can stimulate especially young athletes to think about these core values. Progressing within a sport helps kids and young adults overcome the inevitable difficulties of growing up. Yet, under excessive competitive pressure, the benefits of sport, effort and performance, if not clearly understood, can backfire and consume a young athlete. The pressure of losing, the toil of training and the weight of expectations can easily become overwhelming. Athletes can feel alone and uncomfortable with the responsibility of being talented and the sacrifices that must be made to consistently perform at a high level. These sacrifices are relatively small, yet they demand discipline and will power to follow them through. If you don't know why you are doing what has to be done, you can simply break down in the face of the expectations or an unexpected defeat. Thus, understanding and having faith in the core values of sport helps, especially when everything else is breaking down. And sooner or later, everything does break down.

When children compete for the first time, they obviously have no idea of the core values underlying competition as a form of peaceful human interaction. They have no idea of the formats, the criteria, or how to basically behave in a contest.

In training and coaching programs, it can be very useful to touch the time-honored principles of Olympic competition and fair play. The appreciation and understanding of talent, performance, and human effort as being of equal importance, as victory itself, is not instinctive. It must be taught.

Photo: Quiksilver

Andy Irons pulling into a perfect barrel during the Quiksilver WCT in Cloudbreak – Fiji. This wave challenges the competitors to push the limits over razor sharp and shallow reef; putting surfers in intense and dangerous situations. Nowadays, the WCT venues demand high performance barrel riding, charging big and steep waves or combining 8 or 9 radical and strong moves on one wave! The WCT professional surfers are pushing the sport to amazing new levels, establishing new standards for what it takes to be a pro.

Photo: AJ Neste/Surfing America

USA Surf Team member Tanner Gudauskas' high performance during an early heat at the Quiksilver/ISA World Junior Surfing Championship. Up-and-coming surfers on the WQS or in amateur events have to perform and make the most of small, difficult and usually average or mediocre conditions. Good surfing is good surfing no matter what the conditions.

During an under-14s championship, I witnessed a disappointing episode that showed me the negative impact of valueless coaching (i.e., coaching aimed exclusively towards winning at all costs, regardless of the surfing or performance of the surfer).

In one of the first heats in this under-14s championship, Nicolau was competing against a pretty average surfer and two other kids from another surf school. This was not a team contest.

It seems that the other kids had been practicing blocking and tactical coverages (I'm not sure why they were doing this, if they were still learning how to do cutbacks). So they decided to block Nicolau with 10 minutes to go in the heat, hardly allowing him to catch waves.

Not to be misinterpreted, blocking and tactical coverages need to be learned. They are used in team championships, where points count towards national prestige. Also, sometimes during world championship tournaments, the pros use tactical blocking and strategic use of priority to guarantee wins over their opponents. These are situations that athletes must understand and learn about later on in their junior careers as their surfing improves and the level of competition increases.

During the ISA/Quiksilver World Junior Surfing Championships, two Team USA members – Jeremy and Alex – were up against a lone Australian. With 8 minutes to go, Jeremy was leading the heat, but Alex was still struggling; then Alex caught a great wave and posted posts a high score to turn the positions around: he was in 1st, Jeremy in 2nd and the lone Australian in 3rd.

This was a textbook tactical blocking situation: precious points for Team USA were at stake – no hesitation possible! Head Coach Peter Townend signaled the blocking, and the boys knew what to do. "Latch on to the Aussie, one on each side and don't give him anything!", cried the coach. The minutes trickled down and both Jeremy and Alex manged to keep the Aussie off any potentially good scoring waves (without provoking an interference call themselves), and they both made it. It was a decisive heat and a true sign of team spirit.

The Team USA case represents a situation very distinct from Nicolau's under-14s situation and goes to show that fair play doesn't mean neutralizing competitive instincts; it simply means channeling these instincts to bring the best (not the worst) out of ourselves and our skills. "So never forget that as a professional tactics and strategy can never substitute performance."

Photos: NSL & AJ Neste/Surfing America

NSL's The Game competitive format encourages cooperation between team members and creates a good vibe between all competing surfers. With only one wave counting for each surfer per quarter, giving waves to a team member happens a lot.

Team USA members Jeremy Johnston and Alex Gray congratulate themselves after a more aggressive kind of teamwork. Their cooperation assured precious points for Team USA and was a highlight of the team spirit created by Coach Peter Townend.

Junior surfing talents, like 16 year-old Clay Marzo, can reach very high performance levels. But nothing can substitute the experience and maturity needed to succeed as a professional adult. This is especially evident at the elite level of the WCT, where many of the Top 44 members are 30 years old or more and are still winning contests and competing for the world title. Competitive experience and maturity combined with skill and talent is a deadly combination.

Photo: Quiksilver

In junior age divisions – going from under-10s to under-21s – what is fundamentally at stake is the education and training of potential professional athletes. In other words, the victories of a junior are worth very little if, as an adult, they no longer have the skills and attitude to win.

This takes us down the sad road of junior surfing "burn-outs" – and juniors with unfulfilled expectations. Around the world, history repeats itself: a nation's pride, great skills, loads of trophies – the super junior champion. Meanwhile, all these wins are giving the kid fame and an idea that he/she has already made it as a professional surfer.

Surfing is rock'n'roll, but the reality of the burn-out is a cold reminder of how easy it is to push rock n'roll too far, too high, too soon.

The path towards the burn-out begins by defeats being drowned in sorrow and victory celebrations going on for too long. Problems tend to arise when these reactions to defeat and victory start becoming mechanized habit. Working towards the refinement of skills and the strength of the body to reduce injury occurrence simply aren't on the schedule! Consistently indulging in bad habits or not having good habits becomes the routine. Yet, some surfers stay loose even with these habits – they are always below their potential but talent and pure will-power can go a long way.

Burn-outs can hit athletes afflicted by excessive expectations and strong results as juniors who have lingering problems with confidence and "hunger," which make them unprepared for the natural defeats and extra competitive will needed to surf in the big leagues. These are humbling moments that require strong mental power on the part of the athlete, to allow him/her to bounce back again with confidence.

It is easy to collapse under pressure and not understand the benefits of working a talent, the benefits of relaxing and staying confident, burning but never "burning out." The risk of not making enough effort to work at achieving surfing and training objectives is high with talented surfers. So is the risk of not staying confident or losing the competitive drive necessary to make it in the big leagues. Unconsciously (or consciously), the surfer can become satisfied with the easiness of

Championship sites and waves have varied a lot since the official birth of professional surfing in 1976. Today, the independence of the surf industry allows the most prestigious competitions to take place with small scaffoldings and just fellow competitors, photographers and a handful of spectators watching. Television programs and official websites then share the amazing moments with the world. Mega beach structures near a city or town are still important for spectators to see and meet the pros but thankfully the quality of the waves – not the beach crowd – has become the most fundamental aspect of the WCT.

his/her young glory days, getting stuck in his/her junior accomplishments. The transition to full-time professional and adult competition is always a shock; the question is holding one's ground.

All juniors are at a critical period in their lives where they need different forms of psychological counseling and support, especially when they are subjected to the ups and downs of competition and growing up. Losing is tough, but ignoring the learning potential of a loss is the worst thing a competitor can do.

When competitors don't understand that performing at one's best (and obviously being a good performer) is the most important aspect of competing, then winning is put out of context and the surfer has more difficulty in accepting loss, as well as repeating victories. This is one of the basic core values of sport, one that has been present since the ancient Olympic Games: it is not the victory that is important, it is the effort made to try and achieve it.

Inside and outside the judge's tower – it's inside the contest scaffolding that the judges do their job applying the rules of competition and evaluating high-performance surfing. The judges, seated in independent divisions, apply the performance criteria (from 0 to 10) and adhesion to the adversary (priority rules and interference calls) rules.

When training with João, I witnessed reoccurring cases of talent not substituting effort. The speed with which he learned new moves and new move combinations was truly amazing, but the ability to train hard and be confident to a point of being consistent under competitive pressure, eluded him.

His inability to stick to his training program and his consistent partying/social schedule was a weakness that then plagued his season, especially at international level contests.

Surfers have to play the game: learn to hang-out, understand the party scene, get it out of their system by living it, not ignoring it; then balance that with restraint towards mechanized hanging out habits. Partying is not an everyday, every weekend event; it has to become a special celebration – a celebration (not days of celebration!) of a contest victory, a best friend's birthday (if not the day before a contest) and just apply common sense!

Allocating the merit and rewards to the athletes who follow the underlying values of competition is the basis for the importance of quality judging. Judging must be a respected job taken on by experienced surfers/judges. This helps minimize errors, gives credibility to competitive results, and brings out high performances.

Equality in competition resides in the conditions, whichever they are. Inequality resides in the fame and ranking of certain surfers who will sometimes receive higher points from the judges, while more anonymous surfers will need to surf better to receive the same scores.

The coach's role is connected and even depends a lot on the quality of judging. Since in competition the coach is working to improve the surfer's contest results, learning comes from assuming the responsibility and errors behind defeats, not blaming the judges, wind, tide, surfboard, or anything else. Understanding one's mistakes in a defeat is essential and judges must be part of this learning process.

Judging in surfing is naturally subjective, human and imperfect. A panel of three to seven judges sits down and evaluates surfers' performance, usually for 20 to 30 minutes, according to the modern ASP/ISA criteria of executing radical maneuvers of high difficulty and technical quality in the most critical sections of the wave with power and speed in order to maximize the wave's potential. Innovative, progressive surfing will be valued and taken into account when executed in a determined, controlled fashion. Surfers who abide by these criteria with the greatest degree of risk, difficulty and control in the best waves should be awarded the highest points (on a scale of 0 to 10).

The joy of making the final. Andy Irons wins and begins the celebrations.

There are three basic variables underlying this criteria of evaluating surfing performance in contests: 1) the technical creativity and difficulty of moves; 2) the control, speed, and power in the execution of moves and the flow between moves; and 3) the quality and choice of the wave that allows multiple moves and move combinations to be executed. The better quality waves have the more critical sections and more move potential.

Photos: Quiksilver

Kelly Slater is an example of a creative and spontaneous surfer who made an effort to change judges' evaluation criteria. This freakishly talented Floridian showed the world what trying your best to win can do: it pushes the best even further. Through his desire to make the effort to express himself under competitive pressure, he was successful in contributing to a change in the way in which surfers are judged. He helped motivate more performance, risk and creativity in competition.

After a tight heat in a 6* WQS (World Qualifying Series) contest, Justin gave in his competition vest at the Beach Marshall, took a deep breath and went up to the judges' tower and called, "Head Judge, I need to talk to you." The head judge finished what he was doing and then came out. Justin apologized for interrupting his work, while he grabbed his wife's video camera and showed him all the important waves of the heat. He made the effort to not get emotional and simply show his case to the head judge. The reason he was disappointed was because he had surfed a wave, that in his opinion was worth 8 -8.5 (on the 0-10 scale) but he was scored 7.5. What seems to be a small difference has an enormous effect on the final result. Justin lost to an Australian surfer who caught a wave in the last minute of the heat that was scored 6.5 instead of, in Justin's opinion, a 6.0.

Photo: Quiksilver

Professional free surfing – parallel and alternative to competitive surfing – is also a fundamental component in the growth of the sport that allows different professional options for extremely skilled surfers. Dane Reynolds is an example of the very high standards expected for aspiring professional free surfers.

The Australian's 6.5 and the cumulative effect of Justin's "low" 7.5 turned the result around. Losing like this is very tough, but this well-mannered attitude towards the judges ended up having a positive effect on the rest of his competitive season.

Given the specific, pre-defined and objective nature of the judging criteria for surfers, it ought to be easy to score the athletes' performance. Nothing could be further from the truth! The judges, head judges and technical directors have difficult jobs that constantly test their concentration and objectivity. It's impossible to avoid human error completely. From this point of view, it's easy to understand Justin's outburst. But it was the way he handled the issue that really helped him. The way he spoke to the head judge and used video footage to illustrate what he meant was what allowed him to get around the inherent subjectivity, discuss the errors and discrepancies in the grading of his heat and pave the way for minimizing these errors in the future.

THE SURFBOARD SECTION

To achieve the highest levels of confidence in and out of the water, and for a surfer to perform at his/her best, it is fundamental to trust and feel the surfboard he or she is riding. So with surfboards, don't chase bargains; go for top quality! A good board means essentially a board shaped to satisfy your surfing needs and ability. This depends on knowing what you as a surfer like in a board and eventually having the privilege and skills to communicate and work with a shaper on building surfboards that are continually being refined and adapted to your surfing and the waves you're riding.

Surf Academy's Tip: *To buy a surfboard, be a rational consumer. That means try not to be impulsive. Always go to at least 2 or 3 surfshops and/or 2 or 3 shapers before choosing and buying your board. You might get confused, so be humble with your surfing ability, learn as much as you can from shop owners (and especially shapers) and keep it simple!*

Professional surfing athletes and competitors have boards tailor-made for them and the waves they will be surfing, so it is critical for them to have a basic understanding of how surfboards work and of how they are shaped and measured. Top surfers go beyond the basic measurements of length, width and thickness, contemplating rockers, outlines, bottom contours, fin shapes, fin placements and other subtlties in surfboard construction and function.

Photos: Quiksilver

In this cutback, Dane Reynolds demonstrates the speed and harmony achieved when the surfer, the board and the wave are in tune. Observe the acceleration through the turn! The "magical board" seems to produce these moments constantly.

John had been looking at the surf, waiting for his heat, for more than an hour. He surfed with his 6"3 in the morning. It felt good but was not very fast on his top turns. He had a smaller and looser 6"0, but he wasn't quite sure if it would hold the power of the waves that day. He thought a lot about it but ended up not actually trying out his 6"0 before his heat, so he went out on his 6"3. By the time his heat started, he was tortured with hesitation and when he caught his first wave and did his first turn, he knew it didn't quite have the bite and radicalness that the other surfers in his heat were putting into their top turns. Worst of all, he would spend the rest of his 20-minute heat (which goes by pretty quickly), thinking about his 6"0, instead of focusing on his surfing and waiting for the best waves.

"Choosing a wrong board can easily defeat a surfer. Know as much as possible about your boards and test them before and during competition day."

From left to right: the shaper uses his planer to give form and life to the blank. The laminator, with resin and canvas, protects the shape. The sander tunes and prepares the board for the waves. The painter gives color and more visual impact to the board. Of all the articles and products in the surfing industry, the board is the most essential.

Peter Townend (PT) was invited to be ***Team USA's*** Head Coach in the beginning of 2004. He had the huge task of bringing back pride to mainland America's surfing. Individual talent has always been abundant in the U.S. but that is not the only ingredient of a winning team.

In an interview, in retrospect to his historic Silver Medal in 2004 and in preparation for the 2005 ISA/Quiksilver World Junior Surfing Championships in Huntington Beach, he mentioned how the high technical level of all the team members enabled them to feel confident about their ability to execute and finish various moves on the same wave, and therefore feel confident about their ability to post high scores. But since that confidence could vary in intensity throughout the contest, a

World Champion Sofia Mulanovich shows off her competition weapons. Having a quiver of multiple surfboards increases a surfer's responsibility to test the boards and then choose the right one for the right conditions.

special team spirit and camaraderie had to be created and maintained so that everyone was giving their best at all times. PT attests that was part of the success in the silver medal America won in Tahiti in 2004 and the bronze medal in 2005 maintaining and fostering a positive team spirit makes all team members try their hardest and give their best in each heat.

The correct and efficient execution of *the 7* can lead surfers to pass heats and win contests. Because competitive performance is naturally connected to high-performance free surfing, the best surfers in the world have to strike a balance between being consistent in competitive surfing environments and being creative in free surfing/training environments.

In Tahiti, Pat attempted an ARS (aerial rollo spin/rodeo clown) during a critical moment of his Round 1 heat. A spectacular move, but he hadn't guaranteed his scores and the waves were pretty fickle. The next 10 minutes would pass, and he didn't catch any waves with the potential he needed to pass his heat. He lost but would use the repercharge (second chance) system of the *ISA* world team competitions. Pat recognized right away he had risked too much on that wave and apologized to his friends and fellow team members. Recognizing these mistakes is important in these situations because surfers learn to be more responsible, since their mistakes can jeopardize the team's final standing.

Waves can easily break boards. The will to invest is therefore necessary.

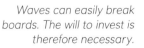

Photos: Carlos Pinto & Pedro Jorge

The Digital Surf Design's (DSD) Surf CAD shape machine: with precise instructions from the shaper, the machine does most of the work, leaving the very important final touches to the shaper. This allows surfers to experiment with more boards and have larger quivers.

Respect for the team as a whole is essential. Athletes are not only competing for themselves but also for their country. So these chosen surfers have to compete and surf at their best, not only for themselves, but also for their country. Taking on this responsibility can really help junior surfers grow up and mature.

Chris was surfing well, but he needed a 4.5 score to qualify and pass his heat. There were only five minutes to go and the tension and stress of having to do something were taking their toll on his mind. The strain was becoming too much at a time when he needed to be focused and calm as he waited for a wave to give him the score he needed. The clock didn't stop ticking, so the tension was visibly mounting. A clearly poor wave came through and Chris was in a position to catch it and, although he still had 2 minutes on the clock, he was unable to let it pass. He caught the wave, made his *take-off*, a solid *bottom turn*, and a good clean *snap* but then the wave closed out. He

Photo: Channel Islands Surfboards

Al Merrick gives his final touches and signs another "magic board."

was given a score of 4.3. Behind Chris' wave was a much better one with potential for at least four or five moves … the wave that he should have waited for. The competitor, who Chris had tried to catch up with, caught it and, without any particularly spectacular surfing, guaranteed his position by not wiping out and scoring a 5.2. He passed the heat, at the expense of Chris' impatience and bad wave selection.

This is a classic example of what often happens in competition and enables surfers to sometimes pass heats with mediocre surfing. Many times the talented surfers are cocky and impatient and don't properly assess the waves and conditions. Then they find themselves unable to catch the better and bigger waves[18] of the heat. A surfer with only mediocre technique can make the most of his or her talent by focusing on catching the best waves.

This means that on the road to becoming a professional athlete, you need to not only work on your technique and surfing skills, but also work on achieving mental control and calm. This mental level can put you in harmony with waves' rhythms and allow you to patiently wait for the waves with the most potential to achieve high scores. Waiting for too long is always an issue but selecting the right wave within the time constraint will always be part of the formula for producing an excellent ride and a winning wave.

Tom Curren, three times world champion and notorious master of the quiver. This surfer's performances are constantly marked by the board he uses and the way in which he flows with the wave on different boards. He is the son of the legendary big-rider and shaper, Pat Curren. The mystical relationship between Tom and his board and the waves, revolutionized competition surfing, elevating him to a supernatural and mysterious threshold.

Photo: João Valente

[18] The Olympic doctrine is based on the ancient Olympic Games in Greece. This doctrine and ideology marked the birth of a competitive, combative spirit extolling the soul and the human will to transcend the humanly possible, peacefully and without violence (stronger, faster, farther). This expansive, combative competitive spirit was typical of warrior nations, but in the Olympic Games it was associated with sport, which is, by nature, a pacific pursuit. This pacific nature of the spirit of sport (marked and respected by the Greeks with a truce from Zeus at the time of the games), created a special aura and attitude capable of expressing and channeling man's animal forces and passions without shedding any blood. Achieving and maintaining this pacific human manifestation and expression was one of the greatest achievements of ancient Greek civilization. It was so universal that the spirit was reborn and flourished for thousands of years later in the west with the first modern Olympic Games in 1896 and is still alive today.

CONCLUSION

More than 2,500 years have brought us to this moment in sport and nothing seems to be stopping its natural development and progress within human societies. So if youngsters take a few years to understand the depth of the values of effort, performance and excellence that make peaceful competition in sports and life so beneficial and useful, it will further guarantee the success of sports.

The role of coaches at this age can be essential in teaching how these basic values, which are the foundations of all professional sports, give longevity and perspective to a career. By not dramatizing either victories or defeats, coaches help to teach sports' core values: correct and harmonious technique; creativity; effort; will and humility. By understanding these values, up-and-coming athletes can become, as adults, responsible (that doesn't mean uncreative!) athletes and balanced human beings.

World-class surf spots serve as natural canvases for great professional surfers to perform their art. Being a witness or a producer of good surfing – or what many consider to be art in motion – is a great pleasure that more and more surfers are able to share. As average skill levels around the world rise, communicating our art is more widespread, but must remain special and inspiring.

Competition surfing plays a big role in spreading our art, so its responsibility towards the correct understanding of sport's competition values is ever more pressing. In surfing, skill, courage and style are some of the most appreciated and recognized qualities of athletes. Competition surfing has sought to favor skill and the natural spectacle of high risk by adapting and refining rules to motivate high-performance surfing[19] as the means to win in competition. Today, the competition structures and criteria followed and developed by surfers, technical directors, judges and head judges are aimed more and more at correctly evaluating and rewarding the skill, risk, power, flow and courage of the surfers. Objective judging is crucial to reward the best riders and rides by giving them the highest points. These are the pillars for spectacular surfing, so the problem is dealing constructively and not destructively with the human error inherent in judging.

---

[19] The best and largest waves of the day, are considered in surfing championships to be those with the most potential and therefore those that bring the highest points.

It is very important to instill these lessons with the younger surfers, especially while they are learning basic surfing techniques, learning to compete in surfing and in life, and learning to take responsibility for their efforts, achievements and mistakes. It is necessary to understand the peaceful values and subliminal ideals of competition: peacefully achieving one's best through maximum effort and personal focus.

Defeats are our responsibility (even if the board wasn't right, the waves were crappy, the conditions weren't ideal, etc.) and it is up to us to learn from them. A friend of mine, Tiago, learned and once told me, "Don't lose, but if you do, don't lose the opportunity to learn a lesson."

The best surfers while thriving to win and consistently perform at their best (ideally surfing to beat themselves and not their adversary) must also make an effort to share and be at peace with other less talented ones when not competing. In surfing, the playing ground – our ocean – is the same for both pros and amateurs.

This peculiar situation in which competition surfing exists – Dane Reynolds has to sometimes share his training ground with Joe Doe – highlights the difficulty of controlling the greed of the more talented and powerful ones when not competing. For those who have reached the cutting-edge of performance, local knowledge and local status, it is important to have respect and admiration for their skills, while also controlling the abuses of these talented surfers towards other less known, less local surfers. Because everyone has the right to express themselves in the ocean.

These are essential ideals, which surfing will hopefully help bring back to sport and society. So that more than defeating our adversary we are defeating ourselves and more than using our skill and power to feed our greed for waves, we are able to be generous, to peacefully share the line-up and the waves.

Wave Selection Drill

Goal:	Select waves that allow the completion of at least 2 or 3 moves
Before going in the water:	*Visualization (5 minutes max.)*: Make surfer visualize (see himself) being patient, allowing close-outs and waves with less potential pass by.
Drill Overview:	*Water* – 2 waves with a 2-move potential minimum *Beach* – Physical conditioning
Duration:	*Water – 1h 20min* = 20 min each session x 4 *Beach – 20 min* = 5 min x 4 *End – 20 minute Heat*
Drill	*Follow these session guidelines:*
(1)	*Water* – Surfer completed 2 (or more) moves in 2 or more waves *Beach* – 10 push-ups/ 10 power leg-jumps
(2)	*Water* – Surfer completed 2 moves on 2 waves *Beach* – Run 1/4 mile/ 20 push-ups/ 20 power leg-jumps
(3)	*Water* – Surfer completed 2 moves only on one wave *Beach* – Run 3/4 mile / 25 push-ups/ 25 power leg-jumps

Surfers who caught two or more waves and completed two or more moves change the next session slightly: now they must continue to select 2 (or more) waves but execute 3 or more moves on the same wave. All other surfers repeat the session exactly.

After the Drill:	20 min. heat or evaluation between the athletes – Best scores for waves with two or more complete moves.

After the training session: Find the time to join surfers and generically discuss competitive goals or their goals for an upcoming surf trip: "Don't forget that in a competition context you need to combine two or more moves to get a decent score … that is what you are training for"; "Not every wave has the same potential, so you must wait for the good ones … even at the most perfect break on the most perfect day – in a contest or in a free surf some waves are better than others – you want to catch the better ones." Creating a wider context for the purpose of the surfer's effort is fundamental for him/her to remember specific goals, as well as to stay focused (over time) on accomplishing them.

"Last 5 Minutes Drill"

Goal:	Use the 5 min time limit to catch 1 wave with at least 2 moves – the "last 5 minutes"
Before going in the water:	*Visualization (5 min. max.):* Make the surfer visualize (see himself) catching a good wave, under pressure, in the last 5 minutes of a heat and completing 2 or more strong moves for a good score.
Drill Overview:	*Water* – One wave (or more) in 5 minutes with at least a 2 move potential/ *Beach* – Physical conditioning
Duration:	*Water* – 15 min = 5 min each session x 3 *Beach* – 15 min = 5 min each session x 3 *End* – 20-minute heat
Drill	*Follow these guidelines*:
(1)	*Wave* – Surfer completed 1 wave with 2 moves in 5 min *Beach* – 10 push-ups/ 10 power-leg jumps
(2)	*Wave* – Surfer does not complete 1 wave with 2 moves in 5 min *Beach* – Run 1/4 mile on the beach/ 20 push ups/ 20 power-leg jumps

Surfers who surfed 1 or more waves with 2 moves in the time limit of 5 min will go out again. They must select 1 wave and execute 3 or more moves in the same wave in the same time limit of 5 minutes.

After the Drill:	20-min. heat using – if possible – other athletes to help judge the heat. Best scores for waves with snaps and a radical move.

After the training session: Find the time to join the surfers and generically discuss the surfers' competitive goals: "You can't give up until the last second … you must maintain positive thinking until the very end of the heat. That isn't easy, but it is the spirit that makes a surfer pass many heats! You must learn to stay positive even under adverse circumstances. That is what you are training for." Creating a wider context for the surfer's effort is fundamental for remembering goals as well as staying focused on accomplishing them.

Judge a WQS/WCT Drill

Goal: Learn to deeply understand judging criteria and evaluate one's own waves.

Before starting to judge: Go over the day's competition framework how long are the heats? How many waves are counting per heat? Any special rules or criteria? Prepare a scoring grid for 10 waves and 4 surfers. Write down the 4 colors (usually black, red, yellow and white) to "name" the surfers and the 10 waves that they might perform on.

Drill Overview: *Beach –* With a pencil or pen and something to write on, judge competing surfers during 2 to 3 heats, following the speaker's announcement of scores during each heat.

Duration: *Beach – 1h* = 20min heats x 3
End – 20 min heat / 1h free surf

Drill *Follow these guidelines:*

(1) *Beach –* Surfers should understand judging criteria and how not all scores are the same among judges. Still an effort is being made to understand judging as a common criteria for evaluating surfing performance and comprehending what the best surfers do to get the best scores.

Surfers should judge 2 to 3 heats in a row

After the Drill: Let the "judges" surf and compete between themselves in a 20min. heat, following the contests.

After the training session: Find the time to join surfers and generically discuss the importance of understanding judging and the level of surfing on the world tour: "Being a judge isn't as easy as it seems … if you want high scores on the 'QS you gotta catch the right wave, rip it apart and make a difference!" Creating a wider context for the surfer's effort is fundamental for remembering goals, as well as staying focused over time on accomplishing them.

Chapter 7

Photo: Patrick Tretz

Randy Bonds from Santa Cruz, California, shows a fundamental part of being a surfer: maximum physical, technical and creative use of our skills, as well as total confidence in ability yet conscious awareness of our humble (not modest) existence. Amongst the power and beauty of nature, surfing is an art form: art in motion. Surfers and coaches must continue to pursue their imagination and passions in harmony with the forces of the ocean.

Conclusions

How to be a surfer embraces the questions regarding being a surfer, growing and developing to be a pro surfer and understanding the important role surf coaches have in increasing the depth and sustainable growth of our sport. The answers are aimed at surfer's sporting, technical and cultural heritage, but could never be exhausted by just one book.

All surfers can be inspired by the legends and myths of the ancient Olympic Games. The most poetic descriptions of the games extol technique, skill, effort, perfection, excellence and eternity, and the heroic acts and words define the

Photos: Quiksilver & Aaron Checkwood/BodyGlove

The ASP finally convinced sponsors to invest in spectacular surfing that means locations with quality waves and always excellent surfers participating. From Fiji, where Danny Wills beautifully times his snap, to Trestles, California, where Adam Robertson busts an aerial, professional surfing is producing a flow of legends and transcendental moments.

essence, the being and the reason for the myths. In surfing, too, the mythical characteristics of the sport, along with the less-known local legends, are born from several of these values. But along with the respect of traditional Western sporting values, surfing can relate to the ancient Polynesian values of harmony and respect for nature.

Surfing's professional athletes represent a balance between Polynesian heritage and ancient Greek sporting values. Competitive and professional surfing is a high-performance sport, an art form of spectacular movement, a dynamic demonstration of beauty, courage, performance and technique. This ideal is achieved by surfers who reach and transcended their personal best during competitions, epic free-surf sessions or riding giant waves. Moments like these, but also the more casual acts, like simply catching and "sliding across" a wave, make the history and the everyday of surfing rich and deep.

When training and closely following advanced athletes, we understand how their spirit, bodies and minds are tested to the limit. *The 7* and its philosophy aim to help prepare surfers for these

The best surfers must master traditional "old school" maneuvers, like the bottom turn, the roundhouse cutback and the power carve, like this one by Bruce Irons. Yet the modern "new school" moves, like the aerial and fin-free snap, are also a necessary part of the repertoire. Bruce Irons is a perfect example of a surfer who mixes "new school" with "old school."

Photo: Tom Carey/ Volcom

This represents the definition of urban beach or wave; therefore, on these beaches there is an apparent lack of waves that is not always resolved in a civilized way.

Surfers have the responsibility to translate and act in the sense of rendering more people conscious of an active universal belief in the possibilities of harmonious human interaction with nature.

difficult moments. These are the moments when it is stimulating to understand the bigger picture in which we all – as surfers and athletes – are inserted.

The 7 is a process of learning and teaching about the ocean, the waves, the more complex wave-riding techniques, and the values with which a surfer should be nurtured – values based on harmony with nature, the ancient Polynesian and Indian philosophies, and values based on trying our hardest to win fairly by bringing out our personal best (the Western roots of ancestral competition as described by the Greeks. *The 7's* philosophies give coaches, parents and anyone interested a framework for the training and educating of ourselves and people of all ages and surf levels. *The 7* is a training method and philosophy that can help and be part of the surfer's education as an athlete and a surfer.

Learning and teaching these values and principles of skill, humbleness, and faith is a great responsibility. A solid, coherent education depends on the quality and experience of the coach (not to mention the support given by parents, family, friends and even schoolteachers).

A young athlete's environment is very complex. It is shaped by home stability, school classroom stability, the quality and quantity of contests and the technical staff in competitions (fundamentally,

Photos: Will Henry

Places isolated from the urban beaches must be preserved and protected from the uncontrolled urban expansion of cities. Through the creation of natural parks, natural heritage classifications and other environmentalist measures, there is a search to actively protect the integrity of these places. These measures work to increase harmony between man and nature. Surfers must make the effort to be the example in the preservation and minimization of man's impact on nature. This attitude is vital for the various generations of surfers to come to be able to continue to travel and find clean, wild places.

the judges and head judge) the atmosphere and level of surfing created by other competitors and athletes, and the spirit and degree of investment by the local surf industry, sponsors and business people. All these factors interact, giving a surf coach a potentially fundamental role in steering the athlete through all the obstacles that exist even in the best athletic environments.

To push and try harder, it seems surfers and all the people envolved in surfing can never stop to believe in the spirit of the sport. To have faith in the example that surfing sets in flowing with waves and the ocean around the world will also help set an example on land with nature and others.

Photo: Patrick Trefz

This faith in the broader values of surfing and surfers in society is at the core of surfers' environmental awareness movement and

Maverick's has become one of the most demanding and incredible waves in the world. Classifying it as a national treasure will help it stay intact and pristine for future generations.

Indonesia is an ideal place to be a surfer. Yet, even here bad vibes from greedy people in a crowded situation can easily ruin the paradise.

the extension of environmental values of harmonious interaction with nature to peaceful interaction among people. Yet, to set the example, things must start by improving surfers' etiquette, especially under crowded situations. Surfing education,[20] to be real, must be lived and followed by example, not by preaching and theorizing.

There should continue to be a will to follow and teach basic (and loose) principles that contribute towards peace in the line-up and the formation of a surfer's education. We are not limiting surfers' freedom. We are not cataloging, packaging and selling surfers' souls. This unfortunately inevitable interpretation is closed and limited because if we are to share surfing's stoke, it has to be done in a sustainable, respectful and thoughtful manner. Uncivilized and unmeasured growth does bring abundance and wealth to those who reap certain opportunities. That wealth must be spread to the roots of the sport and people must be educated to be patient in a crowded line-up but also be respected and not kept in ignorance as a form of the established maintaining power. This is a big part of the problem behind wars' greed and unwillingness to change. This change and outlook at our line-ups can hopefully help surfers and non-surfers be more tolerante and respectful.

Professional contests and the preparation for competing in championships where you directly represent your country, like the World Surfing Games (WSG) and the World Junior Surfing Championships (WJSC) organized by the International Surfing Association (ISA), produce peaceful interaction among nations based on the extraordinary performances of their athletes.

---

[20] Reference to surfing education in the Introduction.

I believe that surfers are examples of how, even as high-performance, world-class athletes, to show an understanding towards the harmonious yet brutal mystique of nature. The need to be open and respectful towards other forms of being and living embodies the values of flow, balance and harmony that characterize surfing.

A surfer can demonstrate, by his or her example, that it is possible to be open, generous and tolerant with solid values and beliefs, while still being competitive and even materially rewarded for making the effort to push personal and human limits.

"How do surfers have an advantage in pursuing this mission?" you may ask. Surfers seek and often find something divine, beautiful and harmonious in what they do because, in the words of Drew Kampion, "surfing as an expression and example of the essential relationship between man and nature [...] is unique in its clarity. This relationship could not be more graphic, more archetypal and symbolic than in the act of catching a wave."

Being a surfer is a way of living and being that meets a transcendental ideal, which is the surfer's communion with nature. Based on this, surfing contributes to the foundations of a global culture – a more united, harmonious, peaceful, and spiritually developed world culture.

In what we have learned in **how to be a surfer**, we can see that understanding the technical and sporting side of surfing is, in itself, a complex, long but fruitful path. But sur-fing's role really goes beyond sport ... that is why all surfers should be aware that the search *to be* is an infinite and divine journey.

APPENDIX
The Coach's Advanced Surfing Drills Checklist

1) *Establish drill duration:* 20-30 min maximum.

2) *Visualization of the move or move combination before the drill:* Study photo sequences, memorize certain chosen parts of a surf movie and understand the move descriptions of *the 7*. This will help the surfer to achieve "real" visualization and then actual execution of the different moves.

3) *Filming surf drills:* It is very important for the surfer to see his/her mistakes to help him/her better execute the different moves in the future. By remembering the feeling of a well-executed move, you remember what you have to do to surf well. This fact deepens your instinct. Visualizing one's surfing helps the athlete to learn the right instincts and feelings and that allow deep technical knowledge.

4) *The reward/ "punishment" incentives established before each drill and executed as part of the drill:* This makes drills more physical but fun and helps surfers to be increasingly conditioned and fit. Incentives are very important to keep motivation and effort levels high. Lack of effort is also any drill's worse enemy.

5) *Practice and effort:* These essential ethical concepts that the surf coach must transmit to the athlete. Falling, but trying again and understanding where and why you fell, is a very large part of learning how to surf. Persistence is the essence of practice, and it requires effort from the athlete to be organized and disciplined in attending and executing consistent training sessions.

6) *Age and number:* It is very important to establish beforehand the age and number of the students participating in each training session. In advanced surfing drills, no more than 5 surfers should be in the water per coach. Create groups based on, for example, these age categories: [6- 10], [10-15], [15-19], [19-35], [35 +].

7) *Surf level:* The coach has to guarantee mutual respect among members of each training session. This comes pretty naturally if all group members have a similar surfing level. So a 12-year-old in a [15-19] group is perfectly possible, as it is a 16-year-old in a [10-15] group as long as surfing levels are compatible.

8) *Different beaches and pointbreaks:* The surf coach's experience and local know-how is very important; it is essential to choose the appropriate waves and wave sizes to train: 1) certain moves; 2) certain combinations of moves; and 3) specific competitive situations.

Surf Drill Tip: Surfing at different beaches and pointbreaks is very important. The contribution of the surf coach's experience and local know-how can be essential to choose the appropriate waves, the crowd levels and size of waves to train on. The coach's goals and choice of moves and combinations that make up a drill or a technical training session have to be consistent with wave conditions and the surfing level of the students: fast, closing-out waves are ok for S turns and barrel combinations but basically impossible to train roundhouse cutbacks; mushier and slower waves are ideal for roundhouses, cutbacks and snap combinations but impossible for a barrel-air combo; pointbreaks are an essential source of move combination and flow training; beachbreaks are essential for competitive surfing training, etc.

Glossary

Aerial	advanced 7 move that involves the surfer's motion, in flight, above the lip line.
Aerial ally-oop	radical 360° aerial (see "normal" 360°).
Aerial reverse 360°	radical aerial that uses 360° rotation in the opposite direction of the ally-oop.
ASP	Association of Surfing Professionals, the official international organization of surfing professionals and their interests.
Backside	the surfer's position on a wave, when his back is turned to the wave. The 7 is equally performed going backside and frontside (opposite of backside).
Barrel	the ultimate surfing move, the seventh of the 7: the surfer travels within the wave at maximum speed.
Beachbreak	a wave breaking over a sand bottom.
Blank	the foamy material from which surfboards are shaped.
Bottom turn	a 7 move, consisting of a drawn-out and continuous turn at the base of the wave.
Beach marshall	member of a contest staff team responsible for giving competitors their heat jerseys.
Channel	area in the surf where there are no breaking waves, allowing easy access to the outside.
Closeout wave	wave that breaks without a rideable section.
Critical section	the most vertical and powerful part of a breaking wave.
Combination or sequence of moves	execution of at least two or three different moves on a wave
Deck	surface of board upon which the surfer supports his feet.
Dings	small dents and tears in the surfboards' surface.
Drop	the act descending the wave from top to bottom.
Dropping-in	descending the wave from top to bottom.
Drop-in on a surfer	the act of "stealing" a fellow surfer's wave.
Duck dive	the way surfers pass under a breaking wave; inspired by how ducks effortlessly submerge under oncoming waves without losing their position or being dragged underwater.
Fin	a thin foil attached towards the tail of the surfboard to give it direction as it moves through the water. The fins are usually below the surfer's back foot, and there are many shapes and combinations available.
Flow	a harmonious surfing style with smooth transitions between moves.
Free surfing	surfing outside of a competition.
Floater	a 7 move riding the lip of the wave for as long as possible, intending to pass over to the next wave section.
Floater 360°	after riding the crest of the wave, the surfer recovers from this maneuver with a 360°.
Frontside	the surfer is travelling with his/her body facing the wave.

Glasser/laminator	in the surfboard manufacturing process, this person takes the shaped board from the shaper and applies cloth and resin to give the board its hard outer shell.
Glassy	perfect surf conditions where there is no wind and the wave surface is completely still and reflective.
Goofy-footer	a surfing stance where the surfer rides with his/her right foot forward; this surfer will ride frontside on lefts and backside on rights (see also regular-footer).
Grab-the-rail	generally a backside move that involves holding on to the rail with your right hand to guide the board through a steep section of the wave inside a tube.
Grommet	a dedicated young surfer, usually no more than 16 years old.
Hang-five	the surfer moves to the nose of the board and places all five toes of one foot over the edge.
Hang-ten	longboarding maneuver where the surfer places all 10 toes off the edge of the nose.
Half turns	poorly executed and incomplete turns on the face of the wave.
Head judge	member of a contest staff team responsible for overseeing the scoring process of the judges.
Heat	elimination round in a contest, which usually consists of two or four surfers competing against each other.
High tide	the time of day when the shoreline is narrowest. The tides are influenced by the phases of the moon, and there are 2 high tides in a 24 hour period (see also low tide).
In tune (with the ocean)	finding the right rhythm of the incoming waves, catching the best and the biggest in each set.
Inside	part of the surf zone that is closest to land.
Interference	penalty given to the surfer who breaches one or more competition rules during a heat.
ISA	the International Surfing Association, which is responsible for world amateur contests at the individual and national team level. ISA is the surfers' voice before the International Olympic Committee.
Judging panel	group of judges who evaluate surfers in contests.
Kook	derogatory term for a beginner surfer.
Leash	surfing accessory that attaches the surfer to his/her board. It consists of a polyurethane cord with an ankle strap on one end and a board attachment on the other. Leash lenghs vary with the size of the surf and the board.
Lefts	waves that break from left to right (as seen from the beach).
Lip of the wave	the breaking crest of the wave.
Longboard	a surfboard that is 9 feet or longer, usually with a rounded nose.
Low tide	the time of day when more sand or rock is exposed on the beach (see also high tide).
Mental visualization	the surfer's moment of concentration and focus on moves and combinations of moves. Very important for advanced technical progress and flow.
Mushy wave	weak wave, usually without steep sections.

Non-broken wave	a cresting wave that is about to break.
Nose	front part of the surfboard.
Off-shore	wind that blows from the beach to the ocean. Ideal for surfing because it smoothes the face of the wave and usually creates barrelling waves.
On-shore	wind that blows from the ocean to the beach.
Outside	part of the surf zone that is farthest from land.
Paddling	alternated arm movement with cupped hands pulling the surfer through the water, similar to freestyle swimming, used to catch waves and get through the surf.
Pointbreak	wave that breaks over a stable (rock or reef) shelf with a dominant direction (right or left).
Power	the force and speed with which surf moves are executed.
Priority	the surfer who has the right of way by virtue of taking off deepest.
Projection	the speed and momentum with which a maneuver is executed.
Quiver	a surfer's collection of surfboards.
Rail	the long edge of the board.
Reefbreak	Usually a wave that breaks abruptly over a rock or coral reef shelf, the most famous of which is Pipeline in Hawaii.
Regular-footer	a surfing stance where the surfer rides with his/her left foot forwards; this surfer will ride frontside on rights and backside on lefts (see goofy-footer).
Resin	a toxic epoxy material used with cloth to protect the surfboard's foam core. It is applied in the 2nd phase of surfboard production.
Righthanders	waves that break from left to right (as viewed from the beach).
Rip current	strong water movement in the ocean that pulls surfers and swimmers in a given direction, usually the direction of the wind and sometimes away from the beach.
Ripping	surfing in a very radical and impressive way.
Roundhouse cutback	drawn out rail turn with complete direction change, followed by a rebound off the whitewater. This is the most complex form of a cutback and a 7 move.
Sander	in the surfboard manufacturing process, this person takes the board from the glasser and polishes off the excess resin to make a finished board.
Set Wave(s)	the bigger waves of a swell that come with a certain regularity, i.e., "Notice how this set only came with four waves and the next set should take at least five minutes to come. It is a long interval swell."
Shaper	the architect, the one who gives "shape", and establishes the dimensions of a surfboard.
Shorebreak	wave that breaks violently on the shore (inside).
Side-shore	type of wind direction: in this case parallel or sidewards to the shore wind. Not ideal for surfing.
Single-fin	board that only uses one fin in the center of the tail.
Skill	advanced control and understanding of surfing techniques.
Snaking	a specific kind of interference call that consists in penalizing the surfer who tries to force an interference on his/her opponent.

Spit	an incredible phenomenon produced by very hollow and tubular waves: a jet of spray "spat" from within the wave!
Speaker	the member of a contest team who comments on surfers' waves, for the benefit of the viewing public.
Spotter	member of a contest staff team who works close to the judge and advises them on what color surfers are catching waves, for example: "Attention judges, surfer in black is catching a wave."
Stoke	very strong will and desire to surf.
Style	the surfer's individual way of surfing and executing moves.
S turns	subtle mid-face rail-to-rail direction changes, used to generate speed. A 7 move.
Swell	the origin of waves; ideally the wave's formation starts thousands of miles away from the coastline and then makes its way to shore, finally transforming into breaking waves, without wind or with off-shore wind. For example, today I saw the surf report and a big northwest swell is arriving and the winds are only going to be between 2 and 3 knots – glassy conditions!"
Tail	back end of the board, which has many variations to adapt to surfers' preferences and surf conditions, such as swallow tail, squash tail, round pin tail, pin tail, bat tail, fish tail, etc.
Teamrider	company-sponsored surfer.
Technique	surfer's ability and skill in executing moves and catching waves, e.g., Kelly Slater's precise technique is admired around the world.
Top turns	fast and sharp turns performed in the most vertical and critical part of the wave.
The 7	the seven chosen moves that define the teaching method in this book.
Three-sixties (360°)	trick that consists in rotating the board 360° on the wave face.
Thruster/Tri-fin	surfboard innovation developed by Australian Simon Anderson that consists of placing three fins on the tail: two side fins and one center fin. Today it is still the most conventional form of setting fins.
Trimming	the original Hawaiian art of wave-sliding. The surfer rides perpendicular to the wave's direction of travel.
Tubes	see barrels.
Turns	all changes of direction done using the surfboard's rail.
Whitewater wave	a wave that has already broken. Beginner surfers usually ride them.
Wave face	section of the wave without whitewater.
Wave section	a part of the wave that is breaking.
Wax	is especially made for surfboards to give traction to the surfer's feet.
Wax comb	accessory used to scrape old wax off a board or give it texture for more traction.
Wetsuit	neoprene clothing used to keep the surfer warm in cold water: a layer of water trapped between the suit and the surfer's body retains body heat. Different wetsuit thicknesses are available for a variety of water temperatures.
Wipeout	falling off a wave.
WCT	World Championship Tour, the ASP's elite world tour of 44 surfers.
WQS	World Qualifying Series, the ASP's qualifying tour for the WCT.

Five "V" M4 MX MBM FLYER II MBB FLYER SASHIMI

Channel Islands Surfboards
http://www.cisurfboards.com

CIFISH MSF MSF-G2 BLACK BEAUTY QUAD MSG MG MBG

MTF

M13

TOW-IN

KSMALL

KBOARD

KSTEP-UP

EAGLES WING

WATER HOG

PERFORMER

PERFORMER II

H2000

H4000

CLASSIC

João De Macedo:

João has surfed and competed at the Pipeline in Hawaii and has competed on the European Professional Surfing Circuit. He finished his economics degree in 2000 and founded the Lisbon based surf school Praia Grande Surf Academia. He obtained his coaching credentials in Australia and worked as Portuguese National Coach in 2002 and 2004.

Sponsored by Reef, Von Zipper and ET Surfboards, João first stood up on a surfboard in 1989. Through the years he traveled to Indonesia, Fiji, South Africa, France, Spain, Brazil, Azores, Madeira, Canary Islands, Scotland and England.

He is president of the Sintra Surf Association and a writer for SurfPortugal Magazine. João is married and divides his time between San Francisco, California, and Sintra, Portugal.

Will Henry *(Photographer):*

Will Henry is a photographer, writer, and avid wanderer of the globe. His fine art photography has won numerous awards and has been exhibited internationally. A graduate of Stanford University with a subsequent master's degree in photography from San Francisco Art Institute, he has published numerous magazine articles, and is a regular contributor to the Surfer's Path, Surfing, Surf Portugal and Surf Session. He is also the founder and executive director of Save the Waves Coalition, a non-profit conservation organization that protects the world's surf spots. Visit Will at *www.savethewaves.org*

Devon Howard *(Photographer):*

"In the simplest of terms, trim gets us from one point to the next. Trim occurs when board, body and wave are in perfect symphony; the ride unhindered and at optimum speed. Explosive, fins-free maneuvers are favorites in the surf mag world, and rightly so. The "wow" factor is undeniable. But for me, it's the more subtle moments of trim and the smooth, connective, flowing, on-rail kind of surfing that gets me burning through a brick of fresh rolls (of film)." – *Devon Howard*

Patrick Trefz *(Photographer):*

"Checking out SURFER Magazine, I was very inspired by the work of Art Brewer. He got me interested in surf photography because he showed a lot of different aspects within the surf culture." – *Patrick Trefz*   Visit Patrick at *www.patricktrefz.com*

Carlos Pinto *(Photographer):*

Carlos graduated in photography from the Ar.Co Institute, Lisbon. He is an official ASP photographer for the WQS (World Qualifying Series) in Portugal and works for SurfPortugal Magazine, OnFire, Tres60 (Spain), Surfers Rule (Spain) and Men's Health. Visit Carlos *at www.charliephotos.com*

Ricardo Bravo *(Photographer):*

Ricardo is a free-lance photographer since 1994. He collaborates with SurfPortugal Magazine, OnFire and Surf Europe and is an editor for Surf Europe – Portugal edition.

Mario Belem *(Illustrations):*

Mario graduated in graphic design from the Ar.Co Institute, Lisbon, and worked in graphic design with Portuguese marketing companies Bomba H and DI, having contributed to projects requested by clients such as first league soccer clubs Benfica, Sporting and FC Porto. After free-lancing for two years, he started his own business: The Studio.com Visit Mario at *www.mariobelem.com*

Photo & Illustrations Credits